## RESCRIPT

In accord with the *Code of Canon Law*, I hereby grant my permission to publish *Jesus, Present Before Me: Meditations for Eucharistic Adoration.*

Reverend Joseph R. Binzer
Vicar General
Archdiocese of Cincinnati
Cincinnati, Ohio
March 26, 2008

The permission to publish is a declaration that a book or pamphlet is considered to be free from doctrinal or moral error. It is not implied that those who have granted the permission to publish agree with the contents, opinions or statements expressed.

Cover design by Jennifer Tibbits
Interior design by Jennifer Tibbits

Library of Congress Cataloging-in-Publication Data

Cameron, Peter John.
  Jesus, present before me : meditations for Eucharistic adoration / Peter John Cameron.
    p. cm.
  ISBN 978-0-86716-857-0 (pbk. : alk. paper) 1. Lord's Supper—Adoration—Meditations. 2. Lord's Supper—Catholic Church. 3. Lord's Supper—Meditations. I. Title.
  BX2233.C27 2008
  242—dc22

                              2008011976


ISBN: 978-0-86716-857-0

Published by Servant Books, an imprint of St. Anthony Messenger Press

28 W. Liberty St.

Cincinnati, OH 45202

www.ServantBooks.org


Printed in the United States of America.


Printed on acid-free paper.


08 09 10 11 12 5 4 3 2 1

For Sister Daniel Marie Fahey, O.Carm., (1927–2007),
who spent her sixty-two years of consecrated life loving the
suffering of the world with her love of the Eucharist.

# Contents

EUCHARISTIC REFLECTIONS
ON THE MYSTERIES OF THE HOLY ROSARY

## *Prayer to Begin Eucharistic Adoration*

Loving Father, your beloved Son has told us, "No one can come to me unless the Father who sent me draw him" (John 6:44). Thank you for drawing me here to the Eucharistic presence of Christ your Son. Thank you for allowing me to come close to the One who has come close to us in the Eucharist—who has become our companion on the way to you. Accept my sacrifice of prayer and the adoration I offer to your Son in the Blessed Sacrament. Unworthy though I am, I come to behold Jesus Christ in this Sacrament of Charity, moved by the certainty that anyone who sees Jesus sees the Father. What impels me to this place is the same hunger that sent the starving Prodigal Son back to the embrace of his father. I come begging for a new beginning. Like those present at the feeding of the five thousand, I have nothing to offer you except my nothingness. But I look to your Son and join him in the thanks he offers to you. I come before the presence of your Son filled with an attitude of expectation. All my life, my heart has cried out with the psalmist, "Lower your heavens and come down!" (see Psalm 144:5). With unimaginable mercy you have answered that plea. I have been made for this presence. May I never be without wonder before the miracle of Jesus present in the Eucharist. Let me relive the surprise of the attraction of Christ. Give me eyes to see beyond all appearances. Make me attentive to the encounter you offer me in this Sacrament. Please help me to offer this time of adoration with all my heart, without becoming weary or distracted. United with the Mother of God, may I ardently adore the Fruit of Mary's womb so that my life may become fruitful in the way that best pleases you and that gives you unending glory. I ask this in the name of Jesus Christ our Lord. Amen.

# EUCHARISTIC MEDITATIONS
# FOR EACH DAY OF THE MONTH

## DAY ONE

# *The Eucharist and the Human Hunger for God*

### WORD OF GOD

*"O God, you are my God—for you I long! For you my body yearns; for you my soul thirsts."* (PSALM 63:2)

### MEDITATION

To be human is to be needy. To be human is to be caught up in a constant search for Something More, the Something More that will satisfy every yearning, every longing, every desire inside us. In fact, the more we realize just how limited we are, the more we see how our whole existence points to something beyond ourselves. In that Beyond is our meaning, our goal. This pining is what moves the psalmist to cry out, "God, it is *you* for whom I long! For *you* my body yearns!"

To be human is to be hungry. But how can the psalmist be so sure that God is the answer? The *Catechism* tells us that "the desire for God is written in the human heart, because man is created by God and for God; and God never ceases to draw man to himself" (*CCC*, 27). God himself places the desire for him in our hearts, and God himself prompts our hearts to cry out to him filled with the expectation of an Answer.

Surrendering ourselves to Mystery—the Mystery of the Body, Blood, Soul and Divinity of Jesus Christ in what appears to be a piece of bread—is the most reasonable thing we can do. Because we were made for this Mystery. We know it deep inside ourselves. It is the way chosen by God to draw us unceasingly to himself. Someone once wrote that "the most beautiful and deepest experience a man can have is the sense of the mysterious…. To sense that behind anything that can be experienced there is something that our mind cannot grasp and whose beauty and sublimity reaches us only indirectly…: this is religiousness."[1] Amazingly, those are the words of Albert Einstein. And if a man so given to science was willing to admit the indispensable need to be religious before Mystery, then we need have no doubt about what we are doing as we come before the tabernacle or the monstrance in worship.

For the yearning for God that God himself has given us is not some idea that we can dismiss, not some feeling that we can repress. It engages one of the most basic drives of our bodies. It is a hunger. And hunger is something impossible to ignore; it has to be answered. The more we give ourselves to God in our human hunger, the more he gives us the Food that makes us divine. God has blessed us with an infallible way to depend on him.

### REFLECTION QUESTIONS

How aware am I of my hunger for God—of my religious sense?

How do I respond when I come to terms with the fact of my neediness? Do self-sufficiency and independence vie to take over?

What are the concrete ways that God is calling me to depend on him at this moment of my life?

## PRAYER

Loving Father, never let me fear the spiritual hunger inside me—
a hunger I cannot satisfy. Help me to see how every hunger is
your gift—the way you lead me to you. In my powerlessness,
may I depend only on you, and in my depending upon you,
may I grow strong in true confidence.

DAY TWO

## *The Hunger of Our Lord*

### WORD OF GOD

*"Then Jesus was led by the Spirit into the desert to be tempted by the devil. He fasted for forty days and forty nights, and afterwards he was hungry."* (MATTHEW 4:1–2)

### MEDITATION

Jesus begins his ministry wracked with hunger. What is the reason for Christ's forty-day fast? Perhaps it was to create in his human flesh a craving that would symbolize the very meaning of his mission. For at the end of the forty days, despite his starving state, Jesus does not cave in to diabolical temptations; he refuses to turn stones into bread. "Bread goes down to suffer hunger" (*CCC*, 556).

Christ's physical hunger feeds his truest hunger. Jesus leaves his fast famished for his Father. He finds his chance to fulfill the Father's will in us. Jesus departs the desert filled with the resolve to impart to all people his own hunger for the Father. In the midst of the ravenous world, he promises, "[W]hoever comes to me will never hunger" (John 6:35). For the hungry who seek out Christ are those best predisposed to receive the Father. Thus, when Jesus meets hungry crowds along the way, he refuses to send them away unsatistfied (see Matthew 15:32). He gives them miraculously multiplied loaves and fishes, and in so doing Jesus feeds them the Father's love. And once their bodily hunger is satisfied, the people hunger to know the source of such a wondrous feast. They see that there is Someone behind Christ's ability to multiply food for them. As Jesus declares in praying to the Father at the Last Supper, "Now they know that everything you gave me is from you" (John 17:7). They hunger to meet this Someone.

At times in the history of the Church, certain persons have been given the charism of *inedia*—the ability to abstain from all nourishment for prolonged periods of time. Among the saints who have received this charism are Alphais, Helen Enselmini, Elisabeth the Good, Lydwina of Schiedam, Nicholas of Flue and Catherine of Siena.

In *The Dialogue* God the Father says to Saint Catherine, "My servants...bind me with the chain of their desire.... I myself gave you that chain because I wanted to be merciful to the world. I put into my servants a hunger and longing for my honor and the salvation of souls."[2] We need a time of spiritual fasting in which union with the Father becomes everything for us. That is why in teaching us to pray "Our Father" the Lord directs us to ask, "Give us this day our daily bread." Our adoration is a sort of "fast" fast. How blessed are those who hunger this way (see Luke 6:20).

## REFLECTION QUESTIONS

How do I respond to the great desires in my life? Do I cave in to what does not satisfy, or do I let my desires lead me to God?

How have I discerned the presence of God in moments of
   great want?
How hungry am I to fulfill the Father's will versus my own
   ideas and plans?

## PRAYER

O Immeasurable Love! Set our hearts ablaze so that we may
more surely conceive a hunger for your honor and the salvation
of souls. (Based on a prayer by Saint Catherine of Siena.)

# *A Presence We Can Approach*

## WORD OF GOD

*"You have approached Mount Zion and the city of the living God...
and Jesus, the mediator of a new covenant."* (HEBREWS 12:22, 24)

## MEDITATION

Pope Benedict XVI makes a point that goes right to the heart of
all human experience. It is this: We need in our lives the presence of what is real and permanent so that we can approach it.
Without that presence, life becomes hard to face. We lose direction. We live a kind of cowering and chaos.

Here is an example. Some years ago someone I know went
to an animal shelter to adopt a dog. There he found a beautiful
three-month-old mongrel that had been abused and abandoned. As he carried the little dog away from the shelter that
night, he could feel her trembling with fear. How could he get
the dog to trust him? Once they got home, he put the puppy on
the doorstep, left the door open and went into the house alone.
From his place down the hall, he called to the little dog. At that
moment the pup was faced with a drastic choice: She could
either remain outside in the lonely and terrifying darkness, or
she could heed the unseen, tender voice that was calling her
inside. The puppy went lurching in. With that, they instantly
became fast friends. The puppy stopped being skittish and

suspicious. She grew playful and affectionate with people. And all because she dared to approach a presence that beckoned her in the darkness.

Jesus Christ in the Eucharist is that real and permanent presence that we can approach. He beckons to us from the silence of the Eucharist because he knows that we cannot be ourselves without his presence to help us. We need a presence that will take us by the hand and lead us out of our isolation and misery. Only a presence—Christ's presence—can reawaken our self, our "I," and give us the courage and desire to live our life to its fullest. The real presence of Christ in the Eucharist saves us from the dread and decay of ourselves. We are made for this presence. That for which we do everything *is* this presence. In faith, we eagerly and lovingly call Jesus "Lord." Why? Because, as the *Catechism* says, it is a sign of "the respect and trust of those who approach him for help and healing" (*CCC*, 448). Jesus in the Blessed Sacrament is the real presence that we can approach in the hope of being transformed, healed and forever changed.

## REFLECTION QUESTIONS

What is the darkness, the resistance in my life that cries out for
a presence?

Where do I hear the voice of Jesus calling me from my fear?

How has my life changed because of the presence of Christ in
my life?

## PRAYER

Loving Father, in the darkness of my misery and fear let me hear the tender voice of your Son. Let me draw close to him, calling him "Lord."

DAY FOUR

# The Eucharist as the Self of Christ

## WORD OF GOD

*"All power in heaven and on earth has been given to me…. And behold, I am with you always, until the end of the age."* (MATTHEW 28:18, 20)

## MEDITATION

The Eucharist is Christ's gift of his body (his self) to us who, every day and in so many ways, face the peril of sin and death. Saint Thomas Aquinas says that Christ would not be so intimately united to us were we to share only in his power. How much better that he should give us his very self, not merely his effects, for the perfect joining of head and members. By his death and resurrection, the Lord does indeed bless us with his miraculous powers (for example, the sacramental forgiveness of sins). But the greatest gift that Jesus intends to impart to us in the Eucharist is nothing less than his very self. For it is Christ's perfect gift of self in the Eucharist that saves us from what is most debilitated and destructive in ourselves.

When twin sisters Brielle and Kyrie Jackson were born prematurely on October 17, 1995, they weighed barely two pounds each. Their doctors placed them in separate incubators and monitored them closely. Kyrie responded well, but not Brielle.

After about a month Brielle's condition radically worsened, and her physicians ran out of things to try. Alarmed by this life-threatening situation, Nurse Gayle Kasparian took Brielle and put her in the same incubator with Kyrie, whom she had not seen since their birthday. Immediately, Brielle calmed down and began to show improvement. Her heart rate returned to normal, her temperature stabilized, and her breathing became regular. Kyrie laid a tiny arm on her sick sister, a photograph of which was reprinted in *Reader's Digest* and *LIFE*, entitled "The Rescuing Hug." What made Brielle better when Kyrie was put with her? It was not simply Kyrie's bodily contact. It was her person, her self, that saved Brielle.

We need the humanity of Jesus conferred to us via Christ's Eucharistic Body and Blood in order for us to become fully human. As the *Catechism* assures us, "Christ enables us to *live in him* all that he himself lived, and *he lives it in us*" (*CCC*, 521). We are longing for this Self in our suffering, our sickness, our help-lessness. We wait for a Body that communicates a Self whom we instantly recognize and who immediately gives us back our health, our well-being, our happiness, our life, our self. One cannot become *wholly* human, Pope Benedict XVI writes, in any other way than by being loved, by letting oneself be loved. In order to have salvation, we are meant to rely on receiving.

## REFLECTION QUESTIONS

In what ways is my self suffering or sick?

Do I let myself be loved by God and others, or do I resist because of self-reliance?

When are the times that I have experienced healing, consolation or wholeness because of Christ's gift of self in the Eucharist?

Loving Father, give me my true self so that I can live all that your Son Jesus Christ lived by his living it in me.

# The Eucharist and Adoration

## WORD OF GOD

*"'Look!' said the king to Daniel, 'you cannot deny that this is a living god, so adore it.' But Daniel answered, 'I adore the Lord, my God, for he is the living God.'"* (DANIEL 14:24–25)

## MEDITATION

Why do we come here to adoration? Because when we are conscious of our self to our core, we perceive at the depths of our self an Other. To be alive as a human person is to be in relationship with Infinite Mystery. That relationship is who we are. And the natural, most reasonable thing we can do once we become aware of this Other is cry out to him. This is adoration.

The *Catechism* says, "adoration is the first attitude of man acknowledging that he is a creature before his Creator" (*CCC*, 2628). "To adore God is to acknowledge, in respect and absolute submission, the 'nothingness of the creature' who would not exist but for God" (*CCC*, 2097). Dominican Father Antonin Sertillanges says, "The sense of adoration causes [the soul] to plunge rapturously into the abyss of its nothingness, and that is the very thing it offers to love."[3]

But adoration is not an act of humiliating self-abasement. Pope Benedict XVI explains that the Latin *ad-oratio* means literally mouth-to-mouth contact, a kiss. Adoration is a way of submitting to divine love—a submission that liberates us deep within. Every time we ardently turn to the divine mystery in adoration, we turn away from crippling self-sufficiency. Father Raniero Cantalamessa, the papal preacher, commenting on the Letter to the Romans, says that the basic sin is *asebeia*—the refusal to glorify and thank God. Fyodor Dostoevsky once wrote that the whole law of human existence consists merely of making it possible for every human being to bow down before what is infinitely great. He said that if a person were to be deprived of the infinitely great, he or she would refuse to go on living and die of despair.

In the Eucharist we have been offered the Infinitely Great, and our response is to bow down before the living God in heart-felt adoration so that we can receive what we need to go on living. For despair lurks at every turn. What we need to be ourselves must be given to us, and we find it in adoration. Father Alfred Delp, a heroic German Jesuit priest who was executed by the Nazis, wrote these astounding words: "Bread is important, freedom is more important, but most important of all is unbroken fidelity and faithful adoration."[4] For "adoration is the acknowledgment that [God] is greater than any human measure, wiser than our greatest wisdom, truer than our greatest truth, more beautiful than our greatest beauty, holier than our greatest holiness."[5]

## REFLECTION QUESTIONS

Do I find in myself a reluctance to spend time in adoration? Why am I slow to spend time adoring the Lord?

What does it mean for me that to be human is to be in relationship
with Infinite Mystery?

How can I more faithfully offer God my nothingness, confident that
the Father wants to be acknowledged by my nothingness?

## PRAYER

Most merciful Father, in the knowledge of my nothingness I
come before your Son in adoration. Free me from whatever
holds me back from offering you constant worship and thanks
and liberate me from within. Let me never doubt the value of
adoration in my life.

DAY SIX

## *This Is My Body*

### WORD OF GOD

*"The bread that we break, is it not a participation in the body of Christ? Because the loaf of bread is one, we, though many, are one body, for we all partake of the one loaf."* (1 CORINTHIANS 10:16B–17)

### MEDITATION

There was a heart-wrenching story in a magazine a few years ago about a baby boy born with a rare genetic disorder that left him with severe deformities; among them, the boy had only one eye. The boy's name was Max. Many people thought the child too frightful to look upon—he should be put away in an institution. His wise mother refused. She saw something exceptional in her son *because* of the abnormalities of his body. She intuited what the *Catechism* teaches: In creating human beings "God... impressed his own form on the flesh he...fashioned, in such a way that even what was visible might bear the divine form" (*CCC*, 704). As the mother put it, "[Max] changes everyone who meets him. He changes their ideas about beauty, about worth. He has made every member of our family...grow up and change their life view in some essential way."[6] This miracle is the result of Max in his own way living out the Lord's words: "This is my Body." The exceptionality of Max's body moves those who encounter him to make a judgment about how they look at all of life. In this respect, Max's presence in the world is "Eucharistic."

When Christ told the crowds, "Unless you eat my flesh and drink my blood, you will not have life within you" (see John 6:53), many people were repulsed at the notion. But for the Lord's true disciples, this summons moved them to look even more closely at Christ's body—to regard it with new eyes and to ascertain its meaning in a more open way—and thereby to see beyond what may have initially repulsed them. They glimpsed the exceptionality of Jesus Christ (an exceptionality conveyed by his body), and they therefore stayed with him.

As the *Catechism* expresses it, "the individual characteristics of Christ's body express the divine person of God's Son" (*CCC*, 477). Saint Thomas Aquinas says that Christ promised to reward his friends with his bodily presence. Even during our pilgrimage he does not absent himself, but through his veritable Body and Blood joins us to himself. We need to hear Christ challenge us with the words "This is my Body" every day of our lives so that our lives may be given new and truer horizons. The exceptionality of the Eucharistic Body of Christ changes our ideas about beauty, about worth. It enables us to grow up and change how we view our lives in every essential way.

## REFLECTION QUESTIONS

What is the standard I use to look at life and make judgments?

What about the gospel do I find scandalous or "too much" for me?

How has staying with Jesus, despite the pressures put on me by the world, changed my life for the better?

## PRAYER

Loving Father, in clinging to the Body of your Son we have life, and in communion with his Body we reach the very heart of God. Make me attentive to the exceptionality of the Body of Christ and change my life so that it becomes a true image of his.

# The Preciousness of the Blood of Christ

## WORD OF GOD

*"For in [the Son] all the fullness was pleased to dwell, / and through him to reconcile all things for him, / making peace by the blood of his cross."* (COLOSSIANS 1:19–20)

## MEDITATION

All it takes is for a detective to discover one drop of blood and a criminal will be convicted for his crime. Conversely, it is all because of one drop of Christ's blood that we who are deserving of an unimaginable sentence are set free. Such is the conviction we live by.

In one of her prayers Saint Catherine of Siena acknowledges how the "high eternal Trinity" reveals divine truth to us "in Christ's blood." This implies that the blood of Christ is something to ponder and behold. For this reason, the *Catechism*, quoting Saint Clement of Rome, implores us: "Let us fix our eyes on Christ's Blood and understand how precious it is to his Father, for, poured out for our salvation it has brought to the whole world the grace of repentance" (*CCC*, 1432). God the Father revealed to Saint Catherine of Siena that the only way for believers to face the fact of their sins is by calling to mind the blood and the greatness of God's mercy. For if self-knowledge and the thought of sin are not seasoned with remembrance of the Blood of Christ, the result is bound to be confusion.

We need the understanding that comes to us through the merciful blood of Christ in order to face the truth about ourselves without self-condemnation. On the night of Passover the Lord kept his eyes fixed on the sprinkled blood marking the doors of the Hebrews in order to save them from the wrath of the destroying angel. So too now, in our Eucharistic adoration, we keep our eyes on the Blood of the Paschal Lamb, for in that Blood is our liberation.

What was it that converted Henry Walpole (who was to die a Jesuit martyr in 1595) from his diffidence about defending the Catholic faith of his birth? When he attended the execution of the great Jesuit poet Edmund Campion, one drop of Campion's blood fell on Walpole's clothes. That single drop confirmed Walpole's sense that the Lord was calling him to follow in the footsteps of the martyr. One drop of blood revealed the truth of the Trinity to Walpole. That solitary drop of blood contained all of Saint Edmund Campion's conviction, courage, resolve—his very self.

The poet Oscar V. Milosz once observed that the Son gives his blood just as the Father spilled his light, so that the descendants of the regenerated Adam would renounce his kingdom of darkness and grasp the identity of blood.

## REFLECTION QUESTIONS

How readily do I face the fact of my own sins?

How have I been affected in my life by others who live out their faith in a courageous way?

What do I want to offer to the Blood of Christ to protect me, to
  increase me, to strengthen me?

PRAYER
Lord Jesus, let your Blood run in my mind as a water of life to
cleanse me from the horror of my sins and to bring forth in me
the fruit of life everlasting. (Based on a prayer by Saint Robert
Southwell.)

## DAY EIGHT

# The Eucharist as Communion

## WORD OF GOD

*"Remain in me, as I remain in you…. I am the vine, you are the branches. Whoever remains in me and I in him will bear much fruit, because without me you can do nothing."* (JOHN 15:4–5)

## MEDITATION

For Jesus, the Eucharist means, "I love you so much that I want to get as close to you as I possibly can. No sacrifice is too great in my desire to express and communicate this love. As I approach my death, it is the communion of love I live with my Father that I want to impart to you."

Why does Jesus make this gift to us? Because we cannot live without communion. As Pope Benedict XVI explains it, men and women need a communion that goes beyond the relationships that they can achieve. We need a unity that reaches deep into the human heart and that endures even in death. In other words, we need a unity that connects us to the Infinite.

But left to ourselves we do not possess the means to bring about such a oneness with God. That is the content of the communion offered to us in the Eucharist. Through communion with Christ, believers gain access to a bond with God that we could never establish by our own power. Pope Benedict says that communion means the fusion of existences: My "I" is "assimilated" to that of Jesus so that I become identified with him in a way that breaks through all the resistant lines of division. Holy Communion closes the alienating distance between God and man. And the resulting unity of love is the one thing that terrifies hell.

Hugh of Saint Victor observes that the devil is not afraid of us when we give alms to the poor, because he himself does not own anything. Neither does he fear us when we fast, because he does not take food. And even when we keep vigil at night he is not afraid, because he does not sleep. But if we are united in charity, of this the devil is terrified, and immensely so, because he realizes that we safeguard on earth what he disdained in heaven. "The Eucharist is the efficacious sign and sublime cause of that communion in the divine life...by which the Church is kept in being" (CCC, 1325).

One day two five-year-old children, both students of the Catechesis of the Good Shepherd, were praying together. One prayed, "Thank you for coming into our hearts, because now we can pray to you inside us." The other child continued, "Yes, He's really great company and we will never be alone."[7] May Holy Communion lead us to live the communion in charity of those two preschool mystics.

## REFLECTION QUESTIONS

What are the main lines of resistance to God in my life?

When have I experienced unity in charity before? How did it change my life?

What can I do practically to be obedient to the Lord's command, "Remain in me"?

## PRAYER

Lord Jesus, through the wonder of the Eucharist, you truly come to dwell inside me. Strengthen my desire for that communion and my confidence that nothing in the world is greater than the union you desire to live with me.

## DAY NINE

# *The Crushing Sense of Absence*

## WORD OF GOD

*"How long, LORD? Will you utterly forget me? How long will you hide your face from me? How long must I carry sorrow in my soul, grief in my heart day after day?"* (PSALM 13:2–3)

## MEDITATION

Sometimes when we pray before the Blessed Sacrament we may experience some disappointment and maybe even shame at the lack of any "sensation" in our adoration. It makes us wonder if we have let God down, if this absence of feeling is a sign of his displeasure or worse, his rejection. In his *Memoirs* the composer Hector Berlioz wrote about "the dreadful sense of being alone in an empty universe," where he suffered agonies, struggling against what he called "the crushing sense of *absence,* against a mortal isolation."[8]

This sentiment is captured by the poet Pär Lagerkvist when he writes, "Who are you who so fill my heart with your absence?/ Who fill the entire world with your absence?"[9] The paradox he voices is amazing. For even when we sense God's "absence," we are overwhelmed with God's presence precisely because we do not "feel" it the way we would like. But look what this experience of spiritual languor does for us: It makes us long for God's presence all the more. The experience of "feeling nothing" becomes a kind of fasting for the Lord's presence. "Love causes a desire for the absent good and the hope of obtaining it" (*CCC*, 1765).

At the same time, the experience shows us how we have nothing to fear, even our experience of "nothing." Because it reassures us that, even when we do not feel Christ's presence in our Eucharistic adoration, we are certain that he *is* there because of our expectation of it, as the poet expresses so compellingly. At the same time, the Lord understands how threatened we feel at the prospect of living the agony of "a mortal isolation." He knows how much that crushing sense of absence terrifies us. That is why the Holy Eucharist is before all else a presence.

As Father Julian Carron, the president of the ecclesial movement Communion and Liberation, likes to point out, we are not ourselves without a presence to help us, lending us a hand so that our truest self will be constantly awakened. We need a presence that will free us from being overcome by the power of nothingness. We need a presence that will save us above all from the decay of ourselves. However, the Eucharist is not an imposing or an invasive presence. Rather, it is a subtle and delicate presence detectable by a docile and receptive soul. Pope Benedict XVI tells us that we must learn that it is only in the silent, barely noticeable things that what is great takes place. That's true of the silence, the stillness and the barrenness of Eucharistic adoration.

## REFLECTION QUESTIONS

How do I respond when I feel overwhelmed by a strong sense of absence, loneliness or isolation?

When has the presence of another at a difficult moment in my life been a palpable sign of God's mercy for me?

What can I do to become more aware of God's greatness in the silent, barely noticeable things of my life?

## PRAYER

Loving Father, when I am overcome by a sense of crushing absence, lead me to your Son in the Eucharist. Do not let me be duped by the lack of sensation in my prayer. Give me receptivity to your Son's gentle presence in the Blessed Sacrament.

# A Begging for Love

## WORD OF GOD

*"Jesus said to Simon Peter, 'Simon, son of John, do you love me?...'*
*He said to him, 'Yes, Lord, you know that I love you.'"* (JOHN 21:15)

## MEDITATION

Every time we come before Jesus Christ in the Eucharist, the Son of God poses to us a question. It is the same question that the Risen Lord asked of Peter after their breakfast on the seashore: "Do you love me?" The Lord knows how prone we are to hide from him because of the shame of our sin, how quick we are to avoid his glance because of our sense of inadequacy and lack of worth. And that is why he consistently "looks us in the eye" in the Eucharist and persists: "Do you love me?"

When Peter denied Jesus Christ three times before the Passion, he discovered something undeniable about himself: Peter realized that his love for Jesus was greater even than all the evil he could commit. There was no alibi, no excuse that could keep him from confessing that love. Christ's question to Peter at the fire makes the apostle realize that there is something indestructible in him, namely, his bond of love with Jesus. Even the atrocity of Peter's sin cannot extinguish the love he has for Jesus—a love which is itself Christ's gift to him. Peter loved Jesus in an invincible way because Jesus first loved Peter in that way.

We need that kind of love to break us out of the blackmail of sin. Christ comes before us in the Eucharist to refire our hope. And that hope, says Father Julian Carron, does not come from what we do but from the awareness that there is Someone who loves us with an everlasting love, who calls us into being every instant, having pity on us who are nothingness. With all our nothingness, we need to put ourselves in front of the Blessed Sacrament in order to rekindle that awareness—in order to let the Lord call us into being.

As Monsignor Luigi Giussani, the founder of the ecclesial movement Communion and Liberation, has pointed out, Christ's greatest miracle was that gaze that took hold of a person's heart, laying bare everything, dismantling every defense. That gaze penetrates our impenetrability; it captures us; it sweeps us off our feet; it reveals to us our true self. The anonymous peasant of Ars understood all this very well as is clear from the way he described his method of Eucharistic adoration to the famous Curé of the place, Saint John Vianney: "I look at Him and He looks at me." Pope John Paul II wisely asked: Were we to disregard the Eucharist, how could we overcome our own deficiency?

## REFLECTION QUESTIONS

How do I respond when I hear Jesus ask me, "Do you love me?"

How aware am I in my daily dealings with the Someone who
    loves me with an everlasting love?

In whom have I experienced the penetrating gaze of Christ? How
    can I foster relationships in which that gaze is kept fresh?

## PRAYER

Loving Father, through the Eucharist, purify me from evil ways; put an end to my evil passions; bring me charity, patience, humility, obedience, growth in the power to do good, defense against all my enemies and perfect calming of all my evil impulses. (Based on a prayer by Saint Thomas Aquinas.)

## DAY ELEVEN
# *Eucharistic Sacrifice*

## WORD OF GOD

*"I urge you…to offer your bodies as a living sacrifice, holy and pleasing to God, your spiritual worship. Do not conform yourself to this age but be transformed by the renewal of your mind."* (ROMANS 12:1–2)

## MEDITATION

When you love someone, you want that love to grow. So what do you do to make sure it happens? If you do nothing at all, what you love will corrupt. Thus, you go out of your way to give yourself to whatever comes first in that relationship—no matter what it is and no matter what the cost. *This* is what Christians mean by "sacrifice." It is not about "giving up things"; it is about doing whatever is possible in order to get as much love as we possibly can. Sacrifice is the way that we eagerly adjust our lives so that our greatest desires come true.

The novelist and Christian essayist Dorothy Sayers observes that when there is something that we supremely want, we never consider the difficulty involved as "self-sacrifice." We view it in that negative way only when we do not *supremely* desire the thing in question. As she comments, "At such times you are doing your duty, and that is admirable, but it is not love. But as soon as your duty becomes your love the 'self-sacrifice' is taken for granted."[10]

The Eucharist is a sacrifice because the Eucharist is Christ's gift of self to the Father in the Passion. Jesus lays down his life in sacrifice so that what comes first in his relationship with the Father will stay first. The fulfillment of the Father's will is what the Son supremely desires. As Pope Benedict XVI says, sacrifice consists in becoming totally receptive toward God and letting ourselves be completely taken over by him. That is what happens to Christ on the cross, and that is what happens to us when we unite ourselves to Christ's Eucharistic sacrifice.

The sacrifice of the Eucharist is what makes it possible for us to love the Father the way Jesus does. In the Eucharistic sacrifice God who gives himself takes us up into his action. Our "participation in the Holy Sacrifice identifies us with his Heart" (*CCC*, 1419). We can love the Father—and receive the Father's maximum love—the same way Jesus does. Thanks to the sacrifice of the Eucharist, our greatest desires come true. We sacrifice for the one we love because through that love we become our truest selves.

Some of the Nazi jailers responsible for guarding the starvation bunker where Saint Maximilian Kolbe was condemned could not believe their ears. They heard the priest praying, singing and comforting the others in there with him—such was the way Saint Maximilian chose to face his self-sacrifice. The Nazi jailers were heard to remark, "That is a man."

## REFLECTION QUESTIONS

What is my conception of sacrifice? Is it essentially something
negative?

What role has sacrifice played in gaining what I supremely desire?

How have I received back a more perfect self by offering myself to
God and others in sacrifice?

## PRAYER

O my God, Trinity whom I adore, let me cling to you in a communion of holiness. Make the whole of my life a sacrifice. May I be completely vigilant in my faith, entirely adoring and wholly given over to your creative action. (Based on a prayer by Blessed Elizabeth of the Trinity.)

## DAY TWELVE

# *The Eucharist as Memorial*

## WORD OF GOD

*"Then [Jesus] took the bread, said the blessing, broke it, and gave it to them, saying, 'This is my body, which will be given for you; do this in memory of me.'"* (LUKE 22:19)

## MEDITATION

One day the father of a family was talking about the birth of his youngest son. He said, "It was an event in the past that does not belong in the past." Why did he say that? Because the event of his son's birth had a special, powerful effect on that father every moment of his life. The more he recalled that event from the past, the more it had a significant impact on the present. That is the Gospel meaning of "memory." "In the New Testament, the memorial takes on new meaning" (*CCC*, 1364).

Memory—memorializing—is what guarantees that crucial events of the past do not remain there but get re-presented in the present. Through the exercise of memory, an action that occurred previously "re-happens." The reoccurring of the past event becomes so real, so immediate to us that it animates and determines our here and now. It shapes the way we think, the way we do everything. For a memory moves us to return to our "source," to what fills our life with meaning. As the author Cesare Pavese put it, "Memory is a passion repeated."[11]

This is what Jesus is asking of us as he gives us this priceless sacrament of love. He is saying: "Do not let what is taking place before your eyes right now fade into the past like some forgotten relic. This event of my handing over my Body and my Blood in sacrifice is the way that your life will become generated, renewed, fortified, perfected. The event will never end in your life if you live that event as a true memory." As Pope Benedict XVI understands it, the memorial constituted by the Eucharist is "the act of entering into that inner core which can no longer pass away."[12] Saint Methodius of Sicily, in extolling the virtues of the martyr Saint Agatha, wrote, "For her, Christ's death was recent, his blood was still moist." He praises the way Saint Agatha lived the Passion of Christ as memory—as a passion repeated.[13]

Understood in this way, we see the radical connection between memory and hope, for it is memory that provides the basis for our hope. Christ at the Last Supper implores us, "Do this in such a way that you will make present in your home, in your family, in your personal circumstances, in your world this unforgettable event of my love. Do this in such a way that every moment of your life will be a constant memory of what happened and what always will happen through me."

## REFLECTION QUESTIONS

What are the events of the past that have a consistent, powerful impact on my present life? What is my hope based on?

What first made me certain that Jesus is the Son of God and my Savior?

How can I live my life so that it is more fervently a "memory" of the Event who is Jesus?

### PRAYER

Lord Jesus, let me live my life as a memory that makes your compassion, your tenderness and your attraction re-happen. Through the witness of my life, may others be drawn to embrace your life.

# The Beauty of the Eucharist

## WORD OF GOD

*"One thing I ask of the LORD; / this I seek: / To dwell in the LORD's house / all the days of my life, / To gaze on the LORD's beauty...."* (PSALM 27:4)

## MEDITATION

It is crucial for us that the Eucharist be "beautiful." Why? Because, as the *Catechism* teaches, it is the human person's "openness to truth and beauty...his longings for the infinite and for happiness," that prompt the human being to question himself about God's existence (*CCC*, 33).

Our fascination with beauty leads us to God. Beauty makes us believers. The playwright Jean Anouilh commented that beauty is one of the rare things that does not lead to doubt of God.

At the same time, our need for beauty shows us the greatness of ourselves—that we are made for something "more." For beauty is a kind of sign that refers beyond itself to something else, and we are designed to detect that. As Monsignor Luigi Giussani, founder of Communion and Liberation, has observed only the relationship with the "beyond," with "something more," makes the adventure of life possible. Our will to penetrate the beyond gives us the energy to seize the here and now. The beautiful is what gives us that will, that energy. In fact,

Giussani continues, the only thing that moves us to say yes to something new that comes into our life is beauty. Only beauty has the power to suppress all our preconceptions, our cynicism, our negativity. Beauty draws out our heart, preventing it from decaying into nothingness.

For beauty possesses a *winning attraction*. What attracts us in something attractive is not the thing itself but the "Something inside something." That is why, in looking at what seems to be a nondescript wafer of bread, we refuse to stop at "appearances." We see the Beyond of the Eucharist...and it is pure Beauty. Saint Bonaventure tells us that in Jesus we contemplate beauty and splendor at their source.

The truest beauty, says Pope Benedict XVI, is the love of God—that is the Something within the something of the sacrifice of the Eucharist. The effects of receiving Holy Communion confirm the ability of the Eucharist's beauty to transfigure our lives. Saint Proclus of Constantinople said that Christ appeared in the world bringing beauty out of disarray, giving it luster and joy.

The Eucharist continues to beautify the disarray of our lives, giving it unimaginable luster and joy. And that is why we rejoice in the words of Pope John Paul II who said that beauty makes one feel the beginning of fulfillment. It seems to whisper to us: "You will not be unhappy; the desire of your heart will be fulfilled."[14]

## REFLECTION QUESTIONS

What were some key moments in my life when I was struck by beauty? How did I respond to them? What impact do they continue to have on me now?

Do I sometimes live in doubt that my heart will be fulfilled?
How have I experienced a connection with the Beyond—with
   Jesus as the Something I am looking for in everything?

### PRAYER

Lord Jesus, the experience of beauty convinces me that I am
loved by Someone who is as great as beauty is irresistible. Let me
surrender myself completely to the attraction I find in you.

# The Eucharist as Communication

## WORD OF GOD

*"May [the Father] grant you in accord with the riches of his glory to be strengthened with power through his Spirit in the inner self...that Christ may dwell in your hearts through faith; that you...may...know the love of Christ that surpasses knowledge."* (EPHESIANS 3:16–19)

## MEDITATION

When we receive the Eucharist at Mass, we "communicate." What is the connection between Eucharistic "communication" and the more common understanding of "communication"? The goal of both is the same: to share ourselves with another. Pope Benedict XVI makes the point that conversation between people comes into its own only when they are no longer trying to express something, but are trying to express *themselves*; then does dialogue become true communication. Along the same lines, the Catholic philosopher Louis Lavelle says that genuine communication takes place only when each of the two persons engaged in the communication "reveals to the other the deep, unknown desire he bears in the secret places of his heart."[15]

Isn't this the very thing that moves us to go to Jesus in Holy Communion? And isn't this the precise reason why Christ deigns to come to us in the Eucharist? As the *Catechism* teaches us, God "wants to communicate his own divine life" to the people he freely created so that thereby they will be "capable of responding to him and of knowing him and of loving him far beyond their own natural capacity" (*CCC*, 52).

Only communication—the deliberate expressing of oneself—can transform us in so radical a way. That is why the communication of Christ's divine life is not limited to the Word but extends to sacrament as well. Dominican sacramental theologian Colman O'Neill says that the presence of Christ in the Eucharist corresponds to our need for communication that is inseparable from love, and that Christ's Eucharistic love establishes that communication because it gives the Spirit of God. Pope Benedict XVI remarks that faith is communication with Jesus that results in a liberation of the self—of my "I"—from its preoccupation with self.

We see an astonishing example of communication as self-liberation in the life of Helen Keller. On that miraculous day when the teacher Anne Sullivan spelled the word *water* into the flesh of the hand of the blind and deaf Helen, for the first time in her life Helen experienced profound communication. Not simply because Helen suddenly understood the dynamics of language, but, as she wrote in her autobiography, "That living word awakened my soul, gave it light, hope, joy, set it free!... I saw everything with the strange, new sight that had come to me."[16] The Word became Flesh, and that Flesh became Food, and in communicating that Food our soul is set free. Such is God's glory: "this manifestation and the communication of his goodness" (*CCC*, 294).

## REFLECTION QUESTIONS

What is the deep, unknown desire for which I seek fulfillment in
the Eucharist?

How have I experienced in my life God's will that I know him, love
him and respond to him in a way that exceeds my natural
capacity?

How concretely have I witnessed God's glory in my life, that is,
the communication of his goodness?

## PRAYER

Loving Father, thank you for the grace of allowing me to be a
regular communicant of the Body and Blood of your Son. May
this priceless gift transform my ability to communicate with
others so as to lead them into a true and lasting friendship with
our Lord, Jesus Christ.

DAY FIFTEEN

## When We Feel Nothing

### WORD OF GOD

*"'Come,' says my heart, 'seek God's face'; / your face, LORD, do I seek! / Do not hide your face from me.... / You are my help;... / do not forsake me, God my Savior!"* (PSALM 27:8–9)

### MEDITATION

How many times have we sided with the psalmist when prayer leaves us feeling forsaken? At times when adoration seems empty, we are tempted to think that nothing is happening, that we are wasting our time. At some point in the life of faith, every believer must "confront what we experience as *failure in prayer:* discouragement during periods of dryness...disappointment over not being heard according to our own will.... The conclusion is always the same: what good does it do to pray?" (*CCC*, 2728). Such discouragement arises whenever we approach adoration from our own preconception about how it should go. We proceed prompted more by emotion than by faith.

But dryness in prayer can be a grace. In fact, God permits periods of dryness as an act of mercy. It is the Lord's way of weaning us from our imagination and feelings (that can easily become idols for us). Dryness detaches us from presuppositions that lead only to an "idea" of God instead of to God himself who is a Person. Dryness of this sort is an invitation to be poor before Christ in the Eucharist. So God permits moments of aridity in our Eucharistic adoration in order to coax us to come before him as a beggar. God delights in the confidence and trust of one who comes before him in utter nothingness, as a beggar, dispossessed of every presumption and of the need to be ruled by feelings. In fact, as Monsignor Luigi Giussani observed, the splendor of God's truth penetrates us precisely in the measure in which one's heart is poor.

There is a nineteenth-century Mexican folktale about a man, crippled from birth, who prayed for years to Saint Anthony for healing. When no cure came, completely frustrated, he went to church and, before the statue of Saint Anthony, yelled, "I begged you and begged you, but you never answered my prayers. You're good for nothing." With that he took a rock and threw it at the statue of Saint Anthony, who *caught* it and cocked his arm to *throw it back* at him. Terrified, the lame man ran out of the church. Then he suddenly realized that his own legs had carried him out. He wept and begged Saint Anthony for forgiveness.

The point of "poverty" in prayer is to persevere. And perseverance is this: to keep seeking the presence of Christ no matter what our feelings may throw at us.

## REFLECTION QUESTIONS

What conclusions do I usually jump to whenever I experience dryness or a lack of sensation in prayer?

What preconceptions or presuppositions do I have about how prayer should go and about how I should feel as a result of prayer?

Is my perseverance ordered to pursuing my own preconceptions and plans or is it my way of seeking the presence of Jesus Christ?

## PRAYER

Lord, let us know what we love, since we ask nothing other than that you give us yourself, wound our souls with your love so that the soul of each of us may say in truth: "Show me my soul's desire, for I am wounded by your love." (Based on a prayer by Saint Columban.)

# Guests of the Lamb

## WORD OF GOD

*"Then the wolf shall be a guest of the lamb…. The wolf and the lamb shall graze alike."* (ISAIAH 11:6; 65:25)

## MEDITATION

Do you know how it came to be that wolves were domesticated? We might think that one day a long time ago somebody came up with the idea of taming a wolf to turn it into a dog. But that is not what happened. The domestication of wolves was not the result of human initiative. Rather, it was a wolf that made the first move. Wolves live by hunting, and hunting is hard. At some point in prehistoric time, some ingenious wolf realized that it was easier to scavenge the scraps of food left over from human meals than to hunt for prey. So the wolf began to linger where human beings lived. And as time went by, the wolf became tamer and tamer until eventually a lasting trust was forged and the formerly fierce wolf became man's best friend.

Something similar happens to us. The more we come close to Jesus Christ in the Eucharist, the more our nature changes. There is an attraction to the Eucharist that we find irresistible, for we were made for this Mystery. Whatever is brutish or untamed about our nature finds its perfection in Christ. "By giving himself to us Christ revives our love and enables us to break our disordered attachments to creatures and root ourselves in him" (*CCC*, 1394).

In the famous story of the savage wolf of Gubbio, Saint Francis of Assisi one day confronted the ravenous beast that had long been terrorizing the town. He reprimanded the wolf for destroying God's creatures without any mercy. But then Saint Francis offered to make a peace pact with the wolf, promising that the people of the town would give the wolf food every day. Mesmerized by the saint, the wolf meekly agreed to this, and thenceforth he went from door to door soliciting food, which the townspeople offered courteously. Two years later, when the wolf died, the people were sorry, and they missed the wolf they had once dreaded. For whenever the wolf went through town, his peaceful kindness and patience reminded them of the virtues and holiness of Saint Francis. An animal that had formerly terrified the people in the end became a creature that they loved, one to whom they looked to be reminded of God's mercy in their midst.

Jesus Christ offers us an even more radical transformation if we will forsake our "wild" ways and be willing to be fed by him. Our transformation will in turn become a cause of hope and assurance for others.

## REFLECTION QUESTIONS

What is unsettled or conflicted in me that needs an answer?

Am I willing to give up my self-reliance and to depend on others for the newness of life I need?

How has Christ's mercy been offered to me when I deserved it the least? What happened as a result of it?

## PRAYER

Loving Father, thank you for welcoming me to the table of the Lamb of God, your beloved Son. May I turn over to him all my willfulness and rebellion so as to live rooted in his ever-tender love.

## DAY SEVENTEEN

# *The Eucharist as Companion*

## WORD OF GOD

*"Two are better than one…. If the one falls, the other will lift up his companion. Woe to the solitary man! For if he should fall, he has no one to lift him up."* (ECCLESIASTES 4:9–10)

## MEDITATION

"In what does man's wretchedness actually consist?" asks Pope Benedict XVI.[17] He answers that the root of human wretchedness is loneliness, the absence of love—the fact that our personal existence is not embraced by a love that makes our existence "necessary." Our misery arises when we live without a love strong enough to justify our existence no matter how much pain and limitation go along with it. What our heart is crying out for is a true companion in whose love we experience how truly necessary and invaluable our existence is.

The very word *companion* derives from the two Latin words *cum*, meaning "with," and *panis*, which means "bread." A companion is literally "bread-with-us"—in other words, everything we need. This literally is the Eucharist! The Eucharist proclaims that God is not a distant fact toward which human beings strive with great effort. "Rather he is Someone who has joined man on his path, who has become his companion."[18]

In the Sacrament of the Altar, writes Pope Benedict XVI in *Sacramentum Caritatis*, the Lord meets us and becomes our companion along the way. True joy, he says, is found in recognizing that the Lord is still with us, our faithful companion along the way. For as Saint Thomas Aquinas pointed out, no possession is joyous without a companion.

Shortly after the terrorist attacks on the United States in 2001, when the airlines were permitted to fly again, a pilot spoke over the loudspeaker to the passengers on his flight, who were naturally somewhat anxious. He said, "For the next few hours we're all going to be family here. So I want you to turn to the person sitting next to you, introduce yourself and tell them a little bit about you. And then I want you to ask them to do the same." By simply asking them to become one another's companions, all their fear faded away.

Christ's presence is the companionship of those he has called like us. "Christ is realized in us and among us through our companionship."[19] Father Pierre Chastelain, a seventeenth-century Jesuit missionary to North America, once remarked that proud Satan cannot bear the companionship of the sons of the true God. That is what we are offered in the Eucharist. The whole great deposit of faith is a treasure we can take with us as a companion, as Saint Gregory of Nazianzus would say (see *CCC*, 256), thanks to the Bread-With-Us of the Eucharist.

## REFLECTION QUESTIONS

What do I do with my loneliness? What judgments do I make about it?

Who are the companions in whom I have discovered God's
tenderness and compassion?
How am I a companion to others? How better can I be the face of
Christ for those in need?

## PRAYER

Lord Jesus, when I am overwhelmed by loneliness, by my limitations, by the anxiety and anguish of daily life, I know that you are with me, close to me in my struggles. In the midst of them, never let me forget or neglect to pray: I need you, Jesus. Come and be my companion.

DAY EIGHTEEN

# Invisible Wonder

## WORD OF GOD

*"[Christ Jesus] is the image of the invisible God, / the firstborn of all creation. / For in him were created all things in heaven and on earth, / the visible and the invisible."* (COLOSSIANS 1:15–16)

## MEDITATION

An expert in the catechesis of very young children has observed that children seem capable of seeing the Invisible almost as if it is more tangible and real than the immediate reality. They can easily penetrate beyond the veil of signs and perceive their meaning as if no barrier existed at all between the visible and the Invisible. Adults, on the other hand, seem to have an inveterate suspicion of anything invisible. If we cannot confirm something via sight and touch, then we grow leery of it.

Yet so many of the things that we rely on the most in life are in fact invisible: sound, oxygen, electricity, the wind, the Internet, love. We never see the gasoline we put in our car. And while it is natural for Christians to grow in their faith "by proceeding from the visible to the invisible, from the sign to the thing signified, from the 'sacraments' to the 'mysteries'" (*CCC*, 1075), we have to wonder where our preschool ability to "see" the Invisible went.

"Wonder" is right—our wonder got worn out. Jesus remains invisible in the Eucharist to reawaken childlike wonder in us. Christ's hidden mode is mercy for us. If we want to be able to "see" him in the Blessed Sacrament, then we need to regain our wonder. And in recovering our wonder, our humanity blossoms in a way it never could otherwise. The theologian Monsignor Lorenzo Albacete makes the observation that wonder is the strongest expression of one's self. When we wonder, we are most attuned to the Mystery toward which our humanity tends. Empirical knowledge cannot lead us to the Infinite. As the great Jewish scholar Abraham Heschel counsels, if we are devoid of wonder then we remain deaf to the sublime. For while ideas lead to idols, only wonder leads to knowing (Saint Gregory of Nyssa).

How, then, can we get our wonder back? The author Cesar Pavese advises that the surest and quickest way for us to restart our wonder is to fix our gaze undauntedly on a single object. At some astounding moment, the object will seem as if we have never seen it before. Wonder is then revived. That is what we have come to do here before the Blessed Sacrament. But the benefits are even greater. The Jesuit poet Gerard Manley Hopkins says that what you look at hard seems to look at you. And Saint Gregory of Nyssa goes one better—he says that we will receive the likeness of that on which we fix our eyes.

## REFLECTION QUESTIONS

How disposed am I to wonder in my life?

What role has wonder played in the things that I know the best?

How have I experienced the wonder of Christ?

## PRAYER

Loving Father, take away whatever is hard or harsh in me. Surprise me again with the invisible presence of your Son in the Eucharist. Let my life be filled with wonder before the mystery of your Son.

# The Eucharistic Imagination of Jesus

## WORD OF GOD

*"The spiritual person, however, can judge everything but is not subject to judgment by anyone. For 'who has known the mind of the Lord, so as to counsel him?' But we have the mind of Christ."* (1 CORINTHIANS 2:15–16)

## MEDITATION

From the first instant that Jesus Christ came to be in the womb of the Blessed Virgin Mary, the Lord began to live his final promise: "I am with you always" (Matthew 28:20). Throughout his life on Earth, Jesus prepared for the everlasting presence he would offer us in the Eucharist.

The Lord's forty-day fast in the desert taught him firsthand that how to be human means *being* hunger and thirst. We starve for truth and meaning; we thirst for what will totally satisfy. No wonder Christ's first parable has as its protagonist a sower whose planted seed promises a hundredfold harvest, or that his first miracle at Cana produces a flood of miraculous wine. As the Lord went about his ministry, he was struck by the certainty of the blind man who could not see Christ's presence but who pleaded for it all the same (see Mark 1:46–52).

Conversely, Christ was overcome by the way absence at the death of Lazarus devastated his sisters Martha and Mary (see John 11:1–44). The onslaught of absence prompted Jesus to make Lazarus present again by bringing him back to life. That event anticipated the real presence of his resurrection which Christ would offer the whole sorrowing world in the Eucharist. The faith of the centurion who declared, "Only say the word and my servant will be healed" (Matthew 8:8) assured Jesus that his believers were ready for an experience of Christ's healing presence that transcends the restrictions of his physical attendance in a place. And when the solitary leper of the ten who had been cleansed returned to Jesus to offer him thanksgiving, the Lord was deeply moved (see Luke 17:11–19). Christ witnessed how powerfully the leper's act of thanksgiving completed his healing and restored his humanity. Perhaps at that moment the Lord resolved to leave us a graced way of offering thanks by which we can be perpetually made new. For the rest of his life, that cured leper lived out of the memory of the day that Jesus healed him; for him it was an event that never ended.

The memorial of the Eucharist remains a moving acknowledgment of Christ's presence that shapes the way we think, feel, act and live. As we adore the Lord in the Blessed Sacrament, we pray that we may receive the Eucharistic "imagination" of Jesus whereby "our way of thinking is attuned to the Eucharist, and the Eucharist in turn confirms our way of thinking" (*CCC*, 1327).

## REFLECTION QUESTIONS

How disposed am I to judge the events of my life according to the mind of God?

What are the patterns in my life that reveal God's desire to be present to me?

How can I be more sensitive to Christ's presence at work in my relationships with others?

## PRAYER

Loving Father, my heart reveals to me that everything that I long for finds its fulfillment in the Eucharist. Attune my way of thinking to the Eucharist so that I will be responsive to the presence of your Son in whatever comes my way.

## DAY TWENTY

# *The Eucharist as Thanksgiving*

## WORD OF GOD

*"Then [Jesus] took a cup, gave thanks, and said, 'Take this and share it among yourselves.'"* (LUKE 22:17)

## MEDITATION

There is a truth that we often forget: We did not make ourselves. We were made. And there was no rule that said that we *had* to be made. Someone decided out of his ineffable mercy to create us. Pope Benedict XVI reminds us that it was only because God knew us and loved us that we were made: "I am preceded by a perception of me,"[20] which means that the most basic and reasonable response of anyone who reflects seriously on the fact of his or her existence is one of *thanksgiving*. For once we become aware of what we have been given, the first, almost automatic, response to reality is gratitude.

If one morning you were surprised to discover a huge bouquet of flowers on your desk, would you not immediately wonder who sent them? And then would you not contact the sender and offer your thanks? In fact, not to acknowledge the bouquet in a grateful way would constitute incivility. When we reflect on the gift of our existence, we realize, as Monsignor Luigi Giussani expresses it, that there is Another in us who is more "us" than ourselves. And if we are not thankful to that Another, we begin to lose something of our very selves.

A priest who has been ordained for over forty years, and who is an acclaimed teacher and writer, for a great stretch of his life was a "hopeless" alcoholic. But then grace came. And he has been sober for decades. It is thanksgiving that gives him his habitual rectitude. He always says, "Anything that we are not grateful for we lose." In one of her writings, Saint Frances Xavier Cabrini states that gratitude for God's benefits is one of the riches of the soul, and that, on the contrary, ingratitude dries up the fountain of divine graces. Conversely, thanksgiving actually increases our humanity.

But how can we, limited as we are, ever dream of offering God thanks that are in any way adequate? The answer is the Eucharist. "The Eucharist is a sacrifice of thanksgiving to the Father, a blessing by which the Church expresses her gratitude to God for all his benefits, for all that he has accomplished through creation, redemption, and sanctification. Eucharist means first of all 'thanksgiving'" (*CCC*, 1360). Monsignor Giussani says that we belong to what makes us grateful. We belong to Christ in the thanksgiving of the Eucharist; we gratefully offer the Father that thanksgiving so that we will belong to Christ more.

### REFLECTION QUESTIONS

Am I a grateful person? Do I thank God daily for all the blessings he gives me?

What makes me grateful; that is, what do I belong to?

What can I change about my life to make sure that I will be faithful in offering thanks to God every day?

## PRAYER

Lord Jesus, offer yourself today for all the evil that we have done against you and for all the good that we have failed to do. And give yourself to us as a sure help in life and in death and as true power with which we will be able to withstand all human evil by increasing in your heartfelt love. (Based on a prayer by Blessed Margaret Ebner.)

# *Eucharistic Worship*

## WORD OF GOD

*"Then I heard every creature...cry out: / 'To the one who sits on the throne and to the Lamb / be blessing and honor, glory and might, forever and ever.'... / And the elders fell down and worshiped."* (REVELATION 5:13–14)

## MEDITATION

Author J.R.R. Tolkien once wrote in a letter: "I put before you the one great thing to love on earth: the Blessed Sacrament.... There you will find romance, glory, honour, fidelity, and the true way of all your loves upon earth."[21] The more we worship the Blessed Sacrament, the more we then grow in the true way of all love.

The *Catechism* tells us that creation was fashioned for the worship of God. In fact, worship is inscribed in the very order of creation (see *CCC*, 347). The world would deceive us into viewing worship of God as something debasing, humiliating. In all truth, worship is our liberation: "The worship of the one God sets man free from turning in on himself, from the slavery of sin and the idolatry of the world" (*CCC*, 2097). Worship is our salvation: "The commandment to worship the Lord alone integrates man and saves him from an endless disintegration" (*CCC*, 2114). Only in worship are we given an adequate way to approach reality. For, as Pope Benedict XVI explains, when we worship God, we drop the fiction that we could ever face God as independent business partners. What do all the multifarious forms of self-worship get us? Misery and dissatisfaction. True worship, says Pope Benedict, means accepting that nothing finite can be our goal or determine the direction of our lives. Rather, we must pass beyond all possible goals. But we need a way to make that "passage"—and that is worship of the Eucharist. When we engage in such worship, Pope Benedict continues, we discover how worship consists in our becoming totally receptive to God, letting ourselves be completely taken over by him. Thus, the essential form of Christian worship, he says, is rightly called *eucharistia*, thanksgiving. In worship, death is overcome and love is made possible. If that is what happens when we worship, why would we refuse?

In a method of religious formation called the Catechesis of the Good Shepherd, preschool children are taught the parable of the Good Shepherd and also about the real presence in the Eucharist. They are then encouraged to meditate on these realities. They pray before a miniature altar on which is placed a chalice, a paten and a statue of the Good Shepherd. In the midst of one prayer session, a five-year-old child whispered, "Let's put away the Good Shepherd statue; there's the bread and wine. It is the same."[22] Such certainty is the fruit of true worship.

## REFLECTION QUESTIONS

How central is worship in my life?

In my experience, how has the worship of God saved me from "disintegration"?

How can I offer a more perfect gift of self to God in my daily life?

## PRAYER

Loving Father, in the Sacrament of your Son I have been given the way of true love. Deepen my desire to worship you and perfect my efforts at prayer so that I will never lose the precious gift that comes to me in the presence of your Son.

## DAY TWENTY-TWO

# *The Eucharist and Friendship*

## WORD OF GOD

*"No one has greater love than this, to lay down one's life for one's friends. You are my friends if you do what I command you…. I have called you friends, because I have told you everything I have heard from my Father."* (JOHN 15:13–15)

## MEDITATION

At the Last Supper, along with the gift of the Eucharist, Jesus gives his disciples another gift: He calls them friends. Jesus is well aware that these are men who are about to betray him, fall asleep on him, desert him, deny him. Nevertheless, Jesus intentionally calls them friends.

A friend, says Aristotle, is another self. Saint Ambrose adds that a friend is a loving companion with whom one is intimately united even to the fusing of souls and forming of one heart. We abandon ourselves confidently to our friends as one would to another self. The persons seated with Jesus around the table of the Last Supper were weak, lacking in courage, plagued with doubt. Yet the Lord chose them—he longed to fuse his soul with theirs. Each of them was to Jesus Christ another self; each was his friend with whom he formed one heart. That is why he gives them his very self in the Eucharist. Despite their limitations, their imperfections, their moral failings, the Lord saw in them something worthy of lasting friendship.

But would they believe in that love? In order to prove that their slavery had been replaced with authentic friendship, the Lord gives them his very Body to eat. What a proof of friendship, exclaims Saint Thomas Aquinas, that Jesus should feed us himself. "In order to leave them a pledge of this love, in order never to depart from his own...[Christ] instituted the Eucharist" (*CCC*, 1337). Monsignor Luigi Giussani remarked that friendship is every relationship in which the other's need is shared in its ultimate meaning.

Jesus knew how much his disciples needed the fortification of his friendship in order to face the needs that would afflict them in the difficult days after his death. "The Eucharist *preserves us from future mortal sins*" because "we share the life of Christ and progress in his friendship" (*CCC*, 1395). It is friendship that unites the apostles in the Upper Room. The spiritual author Monsignor Massimo Camisasca says that Christian friendship is the place of our education in hope. We come together as friends in order to help each other remain in the circumstances in which God has placed us. True friendship is expressed in the way friends help each other to celebrate the presence of Christ.

True friendship, then, is Eucharistic. As a young woman once said at the end of a retreat, "I know that God loves me because he gives me companions."

## REFLECTION QUESTIONS

How much do I value friendship in my life?

Who are my true friends? How have they revealed the presence of Jesus to me in concrete ways?

How can I better devote myself to others' needs in gestures of friendship?

## PRAYER

Loving Father, the night before he died your Son addressed his disciples as "friends." Help me to believe in the friendship that Jesus desires to share with me. Enable me to be a true and faithful friend, especially through my fidelity to the Eucharist.

DAY TWENTY-THREE

# The Eucharist as Belonging

## WORD OF GOD

*"It was not you who chose me, but I who chose you and appointed you to go and bear fruit that will remain."* (JOHN 15:16)

## MEDITATION

What the Holy Eucharist shows me immediately is this: I did not choose God; God chose me. As I gaze at the Blessed Sacrament, I must remind myself that the reason I am here is because Someone loved me first. Being here is not the result of some idea of mine. Rather, something happened to me. I met Someone. And the encounter with him has never ended. He draws me to this place so that I can return again to that first moment of meeting. For knowing that Man has completely changed my life. Nothing in my life remains unaffected by that encounter—not the least detail, the greatest problem, the gravest worry. In the presence I have encountered, everything in my life has met an Answer. As I come before the Eucharist I am positive I have met the Person in whom I was destined to find the meaning of my life.

As Pope Benedict XVI explains it, our "I" realizes itself through a "You." The "You" is Jesus. I belong to him. And the more I surrender to that belonging, the more I become myself.

It is clear to me that the way I feel and the way I see things, the way I perceive and judge reality, come from what I belong to. If we belonged to nothing, we would be nothing. That is why Christ draws us here—to save us from nothingness. In the Eucharist we rediscover the One we belong to who concerns himself with every circumstance, every dilemma of our life. He asks us simply to claim that Belonging.

The night before he died, some ten times Jesus begged his disciples (us) to "remain in me" (see John 15:1–10). He wants us, not because we are perfect, but for one reason only: because we are his (see John 17:6). Consider the story of Maria—a three-year-old Mexican girl with cancer. She was far from home in the pediatric hospital and terribly withdrawn from everyone. One day a catechist told a group of children the parable of the good shepherd. It seemed that Maria was sleeping. But later that night, the nurse heard Maria singing softly: "He knows my name."[23] The Eucharist gives us the assurance of the same belonging. "The principal fruit of receiving the Eucharist in Holy Communion is an intimate union with Christ Jesus" (CCC, 1391). As Monsignor Luigi Giussani would express it, belonging is "having others inside you."

## REFLECTION QUESTIONS

Do I live mindful of the fact that God has chosen me, or do I presume that my life is driven by my initiative?

What are the first experiences of "belonging" that formed my life and made me happy?

How much is independency and self-sufficiency a temptation for me? Who are the people in my life who reveal how much I belong to God?

## PRAYER

Loving Father, you have chosen me through your beloved Son. Increase my certainty of that belonging. By the power of the Eucharist, may that first encounter with your Son be renewed again and again.

DAY TWENTY-FOUR

# The Eucharist as the Bread of Life

## WORD OF GOD

*"I am the bread of life.... This is the bread that comes down from heaven so that one may eat it and not die. I am the living bread that came down from heaven; whoever eats this bread will live forever."* (JOHN 6:48, 50–51)

## MEDITATION

So many things in life simply do not satisfy. We are always searching, longing for that "something" that will give us ultimate satisfaction. The desire for it, the expectation that we will find it is not something that we have given ourselves. That expectation has been given to us. And it reveals to us how, in a certain respect, our hearts are "infallible." Our heart always knows if the thing that captures our attention right now is enough for us. The infallible heart has an uncanny ability to be able to recognize what corresponds to it.

Of course, when still we fail to find what is required for our heart to be fulfilled, we begin to believe that such satisfaction does not exist. We start to distrust our heart—to reduce it or compromise it. We try to convince ourselves that we can be happy by settling for something less than the *totality* for which the heart yearns. But that is to live a lie; that is why we are so miserable. And that is when Jesus Christ comes into our lives calling himself the Bread of Life. This Bread of Life is the "daily bread" that Jesus commands us to pray for in addressing the Father. This bread "taken in the qualitative sense,…signifies what is necessary for life, and more broadly every good thing sufficient for subsistence. Taken literally…, it refers directly to the Bread of Life, the Body of Christ, the 'medicine of immortality,' without which we have no life within us" (*CCC*, 2837).

The sublime film *Babette's Feast* tells the story of a Parisian political refugee who flees to Denmark. There she becomes the cook and housekeeper for two elderly sisters who are part of a strict and rather grim Christian sect. What no one in the village realizes is that Babette is a world-class chef. When she wins the lottery, she uses her winnings to prepare a sumptuous supper for the followers of the sect in gratitude for all their kindness to her. The villagers are used to subsisting on gruel and bland fish soup. When they taste the exquisite meal, their hearts come alive. They become animated, compassionate, gregarious, forgiving. They throw off their rigorousness, join hands in a circle and begin to sing. Babette's feast, patterned as it is so much on the Eucharist, gives them the courage to trust their hearts and to believe that there is Something that corresponds to all their longing. They have tasted the Bread of Life.

## REFLECTION QUESTIONS

What is the "bread" I live by? Is it Jesus or something I have put in his place?

Do I believe that what corresponds to the deepest longing of my heart exists, or have I compromised my desire for happiness?

How have I experienced concretely the satisfaction of Jesus, the
Bread of Life, in my life?

### PRAYER

Loving Father, you have given me a heart that yearns for you.
Through your Son, the Bread of Life, you have satisfied the
thirsty and filled the hungry with good things. May I never
doubt the happiness you desire to give me through Jesus, the
Bread of Life.

# The Encounter of the Eucharist

## WORD OF GOD

*"Behind and before you encircle me and rest your hand upon me....*
*Where can I hide from your spirit? From your presence, where can I*
*flee?... Your hand will guide me, your right hand hold me fast."*
(PSALM 139:5, 7, 10)

## MEDITATION

In the first paragraph of Pope Benedict XVI's encyclical *Deus Caritas Est*, he makes a crucial assertion: Being Christian is not the result of an ethical choice or a lofty idea, but rather *the encounter* with the Person of Christ; this encounter gives our life a new horizon and a decisive direction. In another place, he adds that our initial encounter with Christ finds its source and summit in the celebration of the Eucharist. The philosopher Louis Lavelle observes that the most significant event of most people's lives is an encounter with another who suddenly throws new light upon their lives and changes their direction and meaning. This is the reason why encounter is the very *method* of the Incarnation—God's permanent method. "God tirelessly calls each person to this mysterious encounter with Himself" (*CCC*, 2591). For an encounter makes us wonder what we are really looking for in life.

And the person in the encounter who elicits that question is in some way a key to the answer. We recognize an encounter by the way it never loses its attraction for us, despite the passing of time. An encounter opens wide our whole heart and soul—our "I." It energizes our reason. It reignites our wonder. We can "see inside" things; we are no longer held hostage by our anxiety, our pessimism, our pettiness. An encounter bonds us with something beyond us. It "launches" us, setting our freedom free.

In Flannery O'Connor's short story entitled "A Temple of the Holy Ghost," the main character is a twelve-year-old girl referred to as "the child." She is highly intelligent but also lonely, resentful and mean-spirited. She and her mother go to visit the local Benedictine convent, where they are met by an effusive nun who hurries them down the corridor to Benediction. The child grouses to herself, "You put your foot in the door and they got you praying." But as soon as she kneels before the monstrance, "her ugly thoughts" stop, and she begins to pray, "Help me not to be so mean. Help me not to give my mother so much sass. Help me not to talk like I do." Gazing out the car window as they drive home that evening, the child looks at the horizon and the sun: "a huge red ball like an elevated Host drenched in blood."[24] Thanks to her encounter with Christ in the Eucharist, she sees the Eucharist in everything. The encounter of the Eucharist has given her life a new horizon.

## REFLECTION QUESTIONS

Do I think being Christian is the result of following some idea or moral code, or am I a Christian because I have met Someone in an Encounter?

What were the encounters in my life that have made all the
   difference for me?
How has the encounter of the Eucharist made me reexamine my
   life and set me free?

## PRAYER

Loving Father, in all my fear, my defiance, my resistance, my doubt, the only thing that can save me is an encounter with your Son. Make me attentive to the encounter in the people I meet and in the Sacrament I adore.

# The Mingling of a Few Mere Drops

## WORD OF GOD

*"[Jesus our Lord's] divine power has bestowed on us everything that makes for life and devotion…. Through these, he has bestowed on us the precious and very great promises, so that through them you may come to share in the divine nature."* (2 PETER 1:3–4)

## MEDITATION

A priest once had the good fortune of meeting Blessed Teresa of Calcutta on an airplane. They had an enjoyable conversation. At the end of the flight, Mother Teresa looked at the priest and said, "Father, at Mass when you add those few drops of water to the chalice, think of me." At first the priest was puzzled about the meaning of this request. But then he recalled the prayer that accompanies that liturgical action: "By the mystery of this water and wine may we come to share in the divinity of Christ, who humbled himself to share in our humanity."

Who could doubt that Mother Teresa's heroic apostolate to the poor had become a veritable sharing in the divinity of Christ? What she witnessed to the priest was that the cause of her "success" was her willingness to humble herself in the service of a scorned humanity. As long as her life was given the chance to intermingle with that of the Eucharistic Christ, every miracle of divinity could become possible.

The same is true for us. The *Catechism* assures us that "the fruit of the sacramental life is that the Spirit of adoption makes the faithful partakers in the divine nature by uniting them in a living union with the only Son, the Savior" (*CCC*, 1129). C.S. Lewis put his finger on it: The whole offer which Christianity makes is this: that we can, if we let God have his way, come to share in the life of Christ. As the fourteenth-century Byzantine theologian Nicholas Cabasilas expressed it, we breathe Christ; he becomes food for us. As he blends and mingles himself with us, he makes us his own Body, and he becomes for us what a head is for the members of a body. Thus, the more we put our trust in the promise of that mingling, the greater confidence we gain to face life in a heroic way—to approach life as a godly risk.

When Vietnamese Cardinal François-Xavier Cardinal Nguyễn Văn Thuận (whose cause for canonization has been introduced) was held prisoner by Communists for thirteen years, he was forbidden to say Mass. His could only do so secretly and with nothing but what he had, a few smuggled hosts and tiny bit of wine. Yet, every day he celebrated Mass with three drops of wine and one of water in the palm of his hand. When we offer our life to Christ to be intermingled with his in an offer of total self-giving, sometimes he even permits us to become his chalice.

### REFLECTION QUESTIONS

How readily do I trust in God, handing him over my life to use as he wishes?

Do I believe that I can come to share profoundly in God's life,
    even despite my fragility and my failings?
How has God recently used my weakness to his glory?

## PRAYER

Lord Jesus, let me pour out my life as an offering to you in all humility. Use the littleness of my humanity to the glory of your divinity. May my life become so configured to yours that it becomes a vessel bearing your Eucharistic love to all those in need.

DAY TWENTY-SEVEN

# The Eucharist's True Nutrition

## WORD OF GOD

*"You nourished your people with food of angels and furnished them bread from heaven, ready to hand, untoiled-for, endowed with all delights and conforming to every taste."* (WISDOM 16:20)

## MEDITATION

There's an Italian-American family from Long Island, New York, with an interesting custom. Whenever some member of the family returns refreshed from a vacation, the first thing that the rest of the family asks is, "What did you eat?" Because, for them, the greatness of the vacation can be gauged only by the goodness of the meals. They look to food as the key to the joy that was experienced.

For food does not just keep us alive; its nutrition extends to every aspect of human flourishing. And this is preeminently true of the food that is the Eucharist. But we can forget at times how much our faith relies on the Eucharist for the nutrition we need. And when that happens, we miss the greater nourishment that comes from this Food that we eat and adore. Pope Benedict XVI makes the point that our real food—what truly nourishes us as human beings—is the *Logos* who has truly become food for us as love. Where would we be without this gift of love? Where would we find the energy to take one step more? Pope Benedict XVI says that, in becoming flesh, the Son of God could become bread and in this way be the nourishment of his people who are journeying toward the promised land of heaven. He insists that we need this bread to cope with the toil and exhaustion of the journey. But with the sustenance that the Eucharist supplies comes also a surplus of delight.

This is symbolized in J.R.R. Tolkien's *The Fellowship of the Ring* when elves provide the hobbits (burdened with the duty of saving the world) with a wondrous bread for their long, arduous journey. As one elf comments, "We call it *lembas* or waybread, and it is more strengthening than any food by Men, and...more pleasant."[25] The more we look to the Eucharist for this "pleasantness" and strength, the more we grow in devotion to our waybread. "Growth in Christian life needs the nourishment of Eucharistic Communion" (*CCC*, 1392).

This food is the key to our rejuvenation, our joy. That is why we beg in the third Eucharistic Prayer: "Grant that we, who are nourished by [the Lord's] body and blood, may be filled with his Holy Spirit." That fullness makes others wonder, "What did you eat?" For, as Pope John Paul II assured, those who feed on Christ in the Eucharist already possess on Earth eternal life as the first fruits of a future fullness.

### REFLECTION QUESTIONS

What do I consider my source of sustenance? How much do I rely on the Eucharist to sustain me?

How concretely has the Eucharist helped me in times of trial?

As I reflect on my relationship with God, how has the Eucharist changed my life?

## PRAYER

Loving Father, the flesh of your Son has become real food for us, nourishing and sustaining us. Strip me of all self-reliance, all thoughts of self-sufficiency. Never let me take for granted the gift of the Bread of Life, for I cannot live without it.

# The Fruit of the Blessed Virgin Mary's Womb

## WORD OF GOD

*"When the wine ran short, the mother of Jesus said to him, 'They have no wine.'... His mother said to the servers, 'Do whatever he tells you.'"* (JOHN 2:3, 5)

## MEDITATION

Saint Irenaeus once said that anyone who does not comprehend God's birth of Mary cannot comprehend the Eucharist either. And this makes sense. For, weighed down as we are by the effects of original sin, our tendency is to turn God and faith into an abstraction. The "concreteness" of the Eucharist is given to us precisely to prevent us from that error. And it all begins when God takes on real, human flesh in the womb of Mary, the Mother of God.

Father Raniero Cantalamessa reminds us that the Latin for "mother"—*mater*—comes from the word *materia* ("matter/material"). He says that by silently entering the womb of a woman, God comes down into the very heart of matter, concretely and "really." And the God who became flesh in a woman's womb is the same God who comes to us in "the heart of matter" which is the Eucharist. Moreover, as Pope John Paul II pointed out, not only does Mary lead us to Christ, but also *Christ leads us to his*

*Mother*. As the *Catechism* expresses it, "Mary's function as mother of men in no way obscures or diminishes [the] unique mediation of Christ, but rather shows its power" (*CCC*, 970, quoting *Lumen Gentium*, 60).

A woman named Cheryl Carter-Shotts decided to adopt a young African orphan named Mohammed after learning about his plight while watching television. When the complicated process was at last completed, Mohammed did not understand the concept of "adoption"; he thought he was being brought to the United States to become the woman's servant. Shocked at this, Cheryl said, "I don't want you to be my houseboy; I want you to be my son." The boy replied: "I don't know what that means…but if you teach me, I will learn."[26]

Christ leads us to his Mother so that through her maternal mediation we will learn what it means to become God's sons, God's daughters. She leads us to the Fruit of her womb—the Eucharistic Jesus—whereby we become truly his brothers and sisters. Saint John Vianney says that after the Lord had given us all he could—his Body and Blood to be Food for our souls—he willed also to give us the most precious thing he had left, which was his holy Mother. One gift leads to the other. Saint Germanus of Constantinople called the Blessed Virgin Mary the table of food that fills us who are perishing through hunger with the Bread of Life.

## REFLECTION QUESTIONS

Am I tempted to think of Jesus as an abstraction? Do I find my life being divided by the dualism of "my faith" versus "my real life"?

What role does the Mother of God play in my life? Do I pray to
    her? Do I beg her to make me a true child of God?

Why do I say to Mary, "Blessed is the Fruit of your womb"? How
    does that blessedness affect my life?

## PRAYER

Loving Father, in the Mother of your Son the Godhead is joined
and kneaded into one dough with our humanity so securely
that this union could never be broken, neither by death nor by
our thanklessness. May we always reverence these inestimable
gifts. (Based on a prayer by Saint Catherine of Siena.)

DAY TWENTY-NINE

# The Presence That Vanquishes Death

## WORD OF GOD

*"Now since the children share in blood and flesh, he likewise shared in them, that through death he might destroy the one who has the power of death…and free those who through fear of death had been subject to slavery all their life."* (HEBREWS 2:14–15)

## MEDITATION

Long before Pope Benedict XVI became the Vicar of Christ, he made an intriguing observation. He pointed out that we all share a common fear peculiar to human beings, namely, the fear of being alone in a room with a corpse. Of course, this fear does not make any sense. We know full well that a dead person cannot harm us. In fact, an expired person is less of a threat to us than any of the persons in the world still alive. Still, for many people it is terrifying to be alone with someone deceased.

What can quell that phobia? Not reason, says Pope Benedict. Reason is not enough to overcome such fear. Something else is needed. Really, some*one*. The bout of fear recedes only when we have with us the *presence* of someone who loves us. The moment there is a loving human presence by our side in that room, our fear disappears. We may then even feel silly about ever being scared in the first place. We can face the terror of death when our "I" simply experiences the nearness of a "You."

Christ gives us that presence in the Eucharist to liberate us from our personal terrors. As we are alone in the room of a church with the Body of Christ in adoration, we are blessed by a presence by which every darkness turns light. We grow in the virtue of fortitude that "enables one to conquer fear, even fear of death, and to face trials and persecutions" (*CCC*, 1808). The presence of Christ that we adore is the presence of Christ that we become for others who live their lives in fear, as if alone in a room with a corpse.

After the September 11, 2001, terrorist attacks on the United States, a young priest went as a chaplain to Ground Zero. Dozens of emergency rescuers searched through the debris for survivors…and for the dead. When the remains of a victim were discovered, they were carried into a tent that served as a makeshift morgue. There something amazing happened: Everyone suddenly stopped talking. Without any prompting, they drew close together in a circle around the priest, and they bowed their heads and waited for a prayer. In the presence of the priest, the workers recognized that there was something greater than death in their midst. By our faithfulness to Christ's presence in the Eucharist, we become a presence that liberates others from the slavery of the fear of death.

## REFLECTION QUESTIONS

What are the fears that haunt me in my life right now?

How, in a time of crisis, did the presence of another person make all the difference?

How can I be the presence of Christ to others whose lives are wracked by anxiety and worry?

## PRAYER

Loving Father, when I know the presence of your Son, nothing is fearful to me. The Eucharist assures me that Jesus longs to be close to me in every circumstance, every trouble. Deepen my attention to Christ in the Eucharist so that I will know his accompanying presence at every fearful moment.

DAY THIRTY

# *The Eucharist and Good Friday*

## WORD OF GOD

*"Now is the time of judgment on this world; now the ruler of this world will be driven out. And when I am lifted up from the earth, I will draw everyone to myself."* (JOHN 12:31–32)

## MEDITATION

Why is it possible for us—serenely and with confidence—to make sense of the atrocities of Good Friday? Pope Benedict XVI attributes it to the Eucharistic words of Jesus uttered the night before he died. The pope explains that both the Lord's words at the Last Supper and his death on Calvary are caught up with each other. For if Jesus were to speak the words over the bread and the cup without then going to his death the next day, what meaning could those words possibly ever have for us?

In the same way, the reason why we refrain from regarding the death of Jesus Christ on the cross as "a mere execution without any discernible point to it"[27] is found in the words Jesus spoke the night before in the Upper Room. As gruesome and horrifying as the crucifixion truly is, the Eucharistic words of Jesus imbue us with a new way of perceiving and judging it. On account of the insight provided by Christ's Eucharistic words, we can see inside the event of the Passion and penetrate its deepest meaning. We are able to see beyond what appears to the world as so much shameful failure.

The pope says that what seems on the outside to be simply brutal violence from within becomes an act of total self-giving love. The Eucharistic words foretell that on Calvary violence will be definitively transformed into love, and death into life. With these words we see past the semblance of disgrace and gain access to the act of self-giving love offered from the cross. As Pope Benedict XVI insists:

> Ultimately, the Church draws her life from the Eucharist, from this real, self-giving presence of the Lord. Without this ever-new encounter with him, she would necessarily wither.... Anyone who repeatedly exposes himself to it and confides in it will be changed. You cannot walk constantly with the Lord, cannot ever anew pronounce these tremendous words, *This is my Body and my Blood,*...without being affected by him and challenged by him, being changed and led by him.[28]

Thus, "our Savior instituted the Eucharistic sacrifice...in order to perpetuate the sacrifice of the cross throughout the ages until he should come again" (*CCC*, 1323). We dare to approach that sacrifice with absolute certainty, unscathed by what some take as scandal, enlightened by the Lord's Eucharistic words. And that is why at the start of the Byzantine Divine Liturgy, the deacon—serenely and confidently—invites the priest to begin by saying, "It is time for God to act."

## REFLECTION QUESTIONS

How do the words of Jesus help me to judge my life in a true way?

Where do I draw my life from?

How do I expose and confide myself to the encounter with Christ?

## PRAYER

Loving Father, help me to hold on to your Beloved Son's promise and read his message: Know that I am with you always until the end of the world. That is my protecting wall and garrison. (Based on the writings of Saint John Chrysostom.)

# EUCHARISTIC REFLECTIONS ON THE MYSTERIES OF THE HOLY ROSARY

## *The Joyful Mysteries*

### THE ANNUNCIATION

Being Christian is not the result of an ethical choice or a lofty idea. Being Christian is the result of an encounter with a Person. That encounter begins when the Blessed Virgin Mary pronounces her yes to the archangel and the Word of God becomes flesh in her womb. Salvation becomes a real presence in the world that we can encounter in a human way. Since the time of the psalmist we have begged the Lord to lower his heavens and come down to us. Thanks to the obedience of the Blessed Virgin, that has happened. The encounter that begins at the Annunciation remains the method that God uses to draw all people to himself. It finds its source and summit in the celebration of the Eucharist. At Mass we are like Mary before the angel: We wait for Christ's flesh and blood to inhabit bread and wine. Expecting, we wait for our lives to change.

### THE VISITATION

The Blessed Virgin Mary's journey from Nazareth to the town in Judah where Elizabeth lived was the first Corpus Christi procession. The Mother of God comes to her kinswoman bearing in her womb the Word become flesh. Mary makes her way to her cousin—and to all of us—in order to place in front of us the Mystery that puts to flight all our fear, all our negativity, all our hopelessness. When Elizabeth encounters the presence of Christ in the womb of Mary, the child in her own womb leaps for joy. So too, the power of the real presence in the Eucharist has the power to reach past all our resistance, all our impenetrability and inflame us with new purpose, certainty and gladness. Pope Benedict XVI says that the feast of Corpus Christi is an expression of faith in the fact that God is love. We welcome Mary so that we can be confirmed in that fact.

## THE BIRTH OF JESUS

The star over the stable was the first sanctuary lamp. By its light, angels, shepherds and kings were drawn to Bethlehem, the House of Bread, to adore God-With-Us. In the presence of a baby, even the most hardhearted person changes and becomes tender and caring. But there is an even greater exceptionality about this newborn. "For in him were created all things in heaven and on earth.... / In him all the fullness was pleased to dwell" (Colossians 1:16, 19). In the presence of the infant Jesus we recognize what corresponds exactly to the deepest longings of our heart. Everything that we have been looking for has become flesh and is now lying in this manger. We were made for this presence. All my life my "I" has been waiting to adore this "You." To Christ we say: The fullness of my being is you; my meaning is you. Every time I adore the Blessed Sacrament, Jesus attracts my heart anew.

## THE PRESENTATION OF THE LORD

One of the high points of the Easter Vigil liturgy is the moment after Holy Communion when the Blessed Sacrament is reposed in the tabernacle. Since the end of the Mass of the Lord's Supper on Holy Thursday night, the tabernacle has lain empty and open—bare and abandoned. But now—once again—the "glory of the Lord fills the temple" (see Ezekiel 43:5). The return of the Eucharistic Lord to the tabernacle mimics in a way the moment when the presence of Christ fills the temple at the Presentation of the Lord. The Presentation confirms that Jesus is the firstborn Son who belongs to the Lord. In this mystery Jesus offers us a share in that belonging. God answers our heartfelt cry for meaning, not with mere words, but with a presence in the arms of Mary. What formerly was barren and abandoned in our life is now filled with that presence.

## THE FINDING IN THE TEMPLE

The time when Jesus goes missing prepares us for the days when Jesus will be in the tomb as well as for the days after the Ascension. It is not until Jesus is lost from our sight that we realize how radically our life has been changed because of his presence. Our Communion with Christ has confirmed a truth that we cannot deny: In order to be myself, I need someone else, for alone I cannot be myself. Why? Because when I become conscious of myself right to my very core, I perceive there at the depths of the self, an Other. And I belong to this Other. My belonging to this Other who dwells in my depths precedes any sense of solitude or loneliness I may feel. I was made to be with him. He is the One I am looking for as I search for the missing Jesus. I find him in the temple, in the tabernacle, being about his Father's business.

# The Luminous Mysteries

## THE BAPTISM OF THE LORD

At times even the devout are tempted to doubt the real presence of Christ in the Eucharist. Because our minds are weak, it is difficult to comprehend how what appears to be a piece of bread is the Body, Blood, Soul and Divinity of Jesus Christ. Only little by little did Christ's disciples come to recognize the Lord's true identity as the Son of God. He did not force that knowledge on them at the beginning. Rather, he just stayed with them. He was a true companion to them. They watched and listened and finally became convinced of something exceptional about Jesus that they could not explain. It all began when Jesus, with great humility, presented himself to John the Baptist in the Jordan to be baptized. Then a voice from heaven spoke: "You are my beloved Son; with you I am well pleased" (Luke 3:22). Baptism is a begging for the Father's mercy. As we unite ourselves to Jesus in that gesture before the Host, we will hear the Father assure us: "This is my beloved Son."

## THE WEDDING FEAST AT CANA

In the predicament of the wedding feast of Cana, Jesus faces human need in the thirst of the guests (they have no wine), human expectation in the intercession of his Mother and human fulfillment in the exercise of his divine power. How struck was the Lord by the fact that joy could be brought to a halt due to the want of wine? The thirst that lurked at Cana is the thirst that every man and woman *is*. In changing water into wine, Christ brings forth a veritable flood of it—over one hundred gallons—to convince us that the thirst that we are has been quenched in him. Saint Bede the Venerable said that at Cana the wine was made to fail in order to give our Lord the opportunity of making even better wine so that the glory of God in man might be brought out of its hiding place. That revealed glory remains forever in the Precious Blood of the Eucharist.

### THE PREACHING OF THE KINGDOM OF GOD

From the earliest moments of his ministry, Jesus insists on the link between our need for daily bread and our need for a divine Word. He rebuffs the Tempter in the desert by telling him that we do not live on bread alone but on every word that comes from the mouth of God. And one indispensable Word that comes from the mouth of God is this: "Unless you eat the flesh of the Son of Man and drink his blood, you do not have life within you" (John 6:53). However, original sin constricts our reason and narrows our understanding. We are constantly tempted to think that we can find within ourselves what we need to be satisfied, happy and complete. That is why long before Christ breaks bread at the Last Supper Jesus preaches this word to us. The Eucharist makes best sense to us when we contritely admit that we cannot feed ourselves. As Pope Benedict XVI says, "God's presence in the word and his presence in the Eucharist belong together, inseparably. The Eucharistic Lord is himself the living Word. Only if we are living in the sphere of God's Word can we properly comprehend and properly receive the gift of the Eucharist."[1]

## THE TRANSFIGURATION

On the elevation of a high mountain, in a burst of dazzling whiteness, Jesus Christ is transfigured before his closest disciples. It reminds us of the elevation of the Host at the Consecration and at Benediction. How close is the tie between transfiguration and transubstantiation! The event on Mount Tabor captures our attention, the whole of our "I." We want this beauty never to end, for somehow we sense that it contains everything we have been looking for, everything we need. In the attraction of the Transfiguration we recognize that Christ is something different from everything we have ever seen or imagined. What we could never have thought possible is given to us. Those who freely desire and draw near to this glory experience a transfiguration themselves: We remain human, but we become something more. If bread can become something more than bread—can become God—then our humanity can be divinized as well.

## THE INSTITUTION OF THE HOLY EUCHARIST AT THE LAST SUPPER

Perhaps before the Last Supper Jesus prayed to his Father: "In the days when I fasted in the desert, I experienced in my own human flesh the gnawing of starvation. But bread alone can never be enough for this. No earthly food can satisfy the hunger that the human being is. Hunger is a blessing—a quiet clamoring for You. In our fasting we see how we are famished for the Father. But if You are their craving, what will be their food? Only something that You yourself give them, like manna in the desert. Let me become that, I pray. And then every instant of their hunger will lead them back to You. The persistence of hunger will send them to the Bread of Life. In that Bread that is broken, all will become one, even as You and I are one. Give them this day, each day, this as their daily bread. Can't I become that? I beg you, O Father!"

# The Sorrowful Mysteries

## THE AGONY IN THE GARDEN

Jesus has already celebrated the Last Supper. The Eucharistic mystery now permeates the world. One poignant sign of it is found in what the Lord asks of his disciples in the garden: "Stay here and keep watch with me. Pray with me." Jesus has handed over his Body, his very self to these men whom he calls friends in the Eucharist. As Pope Benedict XVI notes, God has identified himself with man—that is the content of the communion offered us in the Eucharist. And Jesus will not retract that identification as he approaches the Father in his agony of self-surrender. He prays to the Father as the "whole Christ"—Christ and his Church (see *CCC*, 795). Jesus relies on the participation of these chosen ones who are dear companions and priests in order for his prayer to the Father to be complete. Already, they—and we—are implicated in Christ's self-sacrifice. The Lord commands us to keep vigil with him so that we will receive the full measure of mercy meant for those who cherish communion with Christ.

## THE SCOURGING

What has remained concealed from sight since the circumcision of the infant Jesus is now, with the scourging of Christ, plain for all to see: the blood of the Son of God. We need to see this blood. For nothing convinces us of the love and fidelity of friends like their willingness to shed their blood for us. Christ is his blood; we are Christ's because of his blood. With this violent outpouring of blood, we see as well the literal truth of the Lord's words at the Last Supper: "My blood will be shed. It will be shed for you and for all so that your sins may be forgiven." Nothing can keep us from claiming the friendship that Christ offers us at this moment—not even our sins. He sheds his blood to save us from withdrawing into our guilt and shame. That is why God told Saint Catherine that he does not want people to think about their sins either in general or specifically without calling to mind the blood of Christ and the greatness of the Father's mercy. In fact, as Saint Catherine of Siena wrote, "the stones of the virtues are built up with the strength of his blood, for it is by the strength of that blood that the virtues bring you life."[2]

## THE CROWNING WITH THORNS

When the soldiers weave a crown out of thorns and fix it on the head of Jesus, their intent is to mock what they consider to be his pretensions of authority. "All hail, king of the Jews!" they cry, spitting at him. But for those who are sharers of the Lord's Supper, nothing could be more shocking. For in the man who identifies his body and blood with what appear to be bread and wine, we have encountered an authority like no other. Even though we cannot fully understand the meaning of these words, the face of Jesus is filled with a desire that ignites a similar desire in us. These Eucharistic words of Jesus are authoritative in the way that they answer every human need. They open our hearts and make it easy for us to recognize the Mystery we crave. The Eucharistic words of Jesus help us to discover what we aspire to from the depths of our personal poverty. In reviling the authority of Jesus, those who deride him revile the chance for their own happiness.

## JESUS TAKES UP HIS CROSS

When Abraham and Isaac reached the top of Mount Moriah and it became clear to Isaac that he himself was meant to be the sacrifice offered up to God, the Scriptures do not recount that Isaac cried out, protested or tried to escape. In fact, the book of Genesis does not report him speaking a single word. What was Isaac doing, then, in this moment of utter anguish? He was keeping his eyes fixed on his father. For the same certainty of faith that moved Abraham to say yes to this extreme demand of God also moved Isaac to trust his father. Even to death. That is the certainty with which Jesus Christ takes up his cross. He does not endure this load—he embraces it. For the cross is the surest way to the Father. With his eyes on the Father, the horror of every suffering recedes. The Lord offers us in the Eucharist a share in the conviction with which he climbs Calvary. Christ's Body begins to be given up for all at this moment when Jesus takes up his cross.

## THE CRUCIFIXION

Jesus offers his disciples his very Body and Blood in the Eucharist. He then concludes the Last Supper with the words,

"Do this in memory of me." A few short hours later, as Jesus Christ hangs on the cross, abandoned by all but a few, a thief hanging on a cross beside him turns to Jesus and begs, "Jesus, remember me when you enter into your kingdom." This request gives Jesus the Crucified joy, for it is this thief who lives the mystery of the Eucharist. For he lives out the memory of Christ's saving self-sacrifice. The thief begs for the power of Christ's self-offering to flow into his life, even at this late moment on the verge of his death. He begs that Christ's saving death will penetrate and overtake his own ignominious one. The thief lives the Eucharistic memory of Jesus by begging Jesus to remember him. And nothing delights the Son of God on the cross more, because with this memory and the plea to be remembered, Jesus is given concrete proof that he will not die in vain.

## The Glorious Mysteries

### THE RESURRECTION

Jesus Christ rose bodily from the dead. Yet, "this authentic, real body possesses the new properties of a glorious body:...able to be present how and when he wills" (*CCC*, 645). And that is how we can be certain that the Resurrection is a fact that has happened: The Risen body of Jesus Christ has become present in us, the Body of Christ. Nothing else could possibly explain what kept those disparate people—the first disciples—together in the days and years that followed Christ's death. It was not some idea or ideal that unified them; it was the event of Christ's presence in their midst. Even when threatened by perils and persecution, the early Church stayed together because of the undeniable fact that the Risen Jesus had made himself present bodily to his followers in all their weakness, confusion and fear. He drew forth from them Holy Communion. Only the bodily resurrection can effect such a miracle of unity, courage and fidelity.

## THE ASCENSION

If we had not experienced all that we have experienced with Jesus—if we had not been given the Eucharist to memorialize Jesus Christ so that his presence becomes an event that continually re-happens—then the Ascension would be a day of sorrow and dread. As Jesus ascends, he calls us to a new depth of relationship with him. Even though his physical body is removed from our sight, his presence is as close, active and intimate as ever. We access it, not with our eyes, but with penetrating faith. For faith is the acknowledgment of an exceptional presence that changes us. This is not a feeling. Rather, it is a judgment that we make on reality. I know that Jesus Christ is real because of the way my life has changed because of him. The more I use my eyes and heart to recognize those verifications of Christ's presence in my life, the more I am certain that Jesus is with us always, especially in the Eucharist.

## THE DESCENT OF THE HOLY SPIRIT

There is a crucial part of the Eucharistic Prayer called the *epiclesis*. Through this prayer, the celebrant asks God to send down his Holy Spirit so that the Spirit will change the bread and wine offered on the altar into the Body and Blood of Christ. For it is the role of the Holy Spirit to make Jesus present. The mystery of Pentecost reveals to us that what the Holy Spirit did once in the womb of the Blessed Virgin Mary he comes to do again and again in us. For we cannot live without the presence of Jesus Christ. Through the coming of the Holy Spirit, we are given the only power strong enough to shake us to our depths, to clear away our fatalism and to reawaken us to a full and vibrant life. In turn, the Holy Spirit gives us the ability to make Jesus present to others and to the whole world.

## THE ASSUMPTION

We come before the Eucharist waiting for Someone. This expectation is a sharing in the grace of the Assumption. For as Pope John Paul II remarked, the Blessed Virgin Mary teaches believers how to look to the future with total abandonment to God. In Mary we experience how hope has become enriched with ever-new reasons. The Mother of God communicates to God's people a constantly new capacity to await the will of God and to abandon themselves in trust to the Lord's promises. If we were not left with the sacrament of Christ's Body here on earth, chances are that our friendship with Jesus would become strained and abstract. And if Our Lady were to be assumed into heaven without her body, we might begin to feel disconnected from our Mother, maybe even orphaned. The body of Mary in heaven leads us with confidence to the Body of Christ on Earth.

## THE CORONATION OF MARY

To recognize someone as queen is to recognize that she possesses a sovereign power upon which we rely for our own well-being and happiness. As the Blessed Virgin Mary is crowned

Queen of heaven and Earth, we celebrate the fact that the supreme power that Mary possesses is her union with her divine Son. In speaking of Our Lady's queenship, Pope John Paul II stated that Mary's glorious state brings about a continuous and caring closeness. For she is a Queen who gives all that she possesses, participating above all in the life and love of Christ. The Byzantine Divine Liturgy proclaims, "In you, O Woman full of grace, all creation exults.... Glory of virgins of whom God took flesh.... He has made your womb his throne."[3] Mary exercises her queenship by bequeathing us with all she possesses: Jesus, the Fruit of her womb in the Eucharist. There is no greater caring closeness.

EUCHARISTIC DEVOTIONS

# *Eucharistic Colloquy*

## THE CALL OF THE EUCHARIST

The mercy of Jesus calls to us in the Eucharist:

"Come to me, all you who are weary and find life burdensome, and I will refresh you. All you who hunger and thirst for fulfillment, for holiness, come and have your fill of my life as you eat my Body and drink my Blood.

"Come by yourselves to an out-of-the-way place and rest a little. Come into my heart that longs to fill you with my rest, my peace, my love.

"I see many people coming and going making it impossible for you to so much as eat. So come to me, and I will feed you with myself.

"Do you fear that I will not be enough? Do you have doubts that I will understand the depth of your hunger? Do you fret that I will feed only others and overlook you whom I love the most in your littleness and need? Come to me from *that* deserted place in your soul.

"Come, though you think that there is not enough to give even a morsel to the vast crowds. Bring me only what you have: your five barley loaves, your two fish. Bring me your nothingness, your emptiness, your powerlessness. Bring me only that and nothing more. For you have nothing more to offer. And watch me lift your nothingness in blessing. Watch me multiply your offering so that it overflows with my saving presence.

"And upon that you will feast. You who offer me your gift of selflessness will feed on the gift of myself. And the graces of my presence will be multiplied within you so that you become my gift, my offering to the Father. You become my Body whereby God is given to God.

"And then—together—let us gather up the fragments so that nothing will be wasted, nothing will be lost. For it is out of the fragments of your life that I will reveal the fullness of my life so that that fullness becomes yours forever.

"So come to me, come to your Lord—to Jesus. Come to me as I rest in the temple before offering my Body in Eucharist, before offering my life on the cross. Come to me as I watch the poor widow offer her two copper coins in the temple treasury. Accompany me as I witness this offering of self, made with such abandon, in unhesitating faith. Know with me that this act of love is the costliest offering, greater than any sum of silver or gold.

"And now offer yourselves—from your want, not from your surplus. Offer yourselves to me that you might become my living temples. For only when you empty yourselves in my sacred presence can I fill you with that sacrifice that honors your sacrifice.

"Come to me, like Zacchaeus. Come, you who are frightened by the crowd. Come down out of the branches of the tree where you would seek to hide from my glance. Come, you who long so much to be with me, but who think yourself too small, too unworthy. Come down from out of that tree, for it is with you that I desire to stay.

"It is with you that I long to live. Come and be a worthy dwelling for such a guest. But do not try to justify yourself. Only I can make you worthy. You deserve to delight in my presence for one reason only: because I make you worthy of it. Leave behind all your excuses and all your lies. Receive only the justification that the Bread of Life establishes within you.

"Be changed. Be transfigured—as radiant as my face on Mount Tabor, as bright as the Host you behold in elevation.

"Be transformed like the leper with his fetid flesh. 'Lord, if you will to do so you can make me clean.'... 'I do will it: Be clean.' See his body renewed by my touch of healing. And come to me; adore my flesh that changes the death you suffer each day into wholeness and resurrection. See in your body the glory of my transfiguration. Let us be transformed by love into the same Body.

"Come to me like the woman with the twelve-year flow of blood. Come to the physician who heals you with his bleeding. Reach out your hands, but touch my wounds, not my clothing. And taste the blood that unites. Drink deeply of that Precious Blood by which we are united. And let your lives flow only with the Blood of my Heart. And shed that blood, give that blood, for by our union many shall be healed. Be with me as I pour out my blood every day, for in that perpetual flow of blood all will know mercy and forgiveness.

"At the beginning of my ministry, I fasted for forty days in the desert and at the end I was hungry. Satan was ready then to feed me. But I did not want the devil's meal, the food of temptation. I hunger for you, for your trust in me, for your holiness.

"At the end of my ministry, as I hung upon the cross, I cried out in thirst, thirsting not for wine or a swallow of sour vinegar, but for your faith. Only the offer of your self, your willingness to receive the consolation I offer can slake my burning thirst.

"Come to me. Adore my real life, which you cannot see. Come to me, and as you gaze in faith, know that he whom you adore adores God's life within you."

# Eucharistic Litany
## Based on *Sacramentum Caritatis*

In the apostolic exhortation *Sacramentum Caritatis*, Pope Benedict XVI wrote that "the sacrament of charity, the Holy Eucharist is the gift that Jesus Christ makes of himself, thus revealing to us God's infinite love for every man and woman."[1] We pray the following litany, which is based on lines from *Sacramentum Caritatis*, as a way of begging God to reveal that infinite love in our life more and more.

*RESPONSE:* Body of Christ, be my salvation

In the Sacrament of the Altar, the Lord meets us and becomes our companion along the way, *RESPONSE*

In the Eucharist Jesus gives us the totality of his life and reveals the ultimate origin of this love, *RESPONSE*

The Eucharist contains radical newness that is offered to us again at every celebration, *RESPONSE*

Through the Eucharist we enter into the very dynamic of Jesus' self-giving, *RESPONSE*

Through the sacrament of the Eucharist Jesus shows us the bond that he willed to establish between himself and us, *RESPONSE*

The Eucharist is Christ who gives himself to us and continually builds us up as his body, *RESPONSE*

In the most blessed Eucharist is contained the entire spiritual wealth of the Church, namely Christ himself, *RESPONSE*

Jesus, our living bread, gives life to humanity through his flesh, *RESPONSE*

The Eucharist is the sacrament of the Bridegroom and of the Bride, *RESPONSE*

The Eucharist expresses the irrevocable nature of God's love in Christ for his Church, *RESPONSE*

Our wounded nature would go astray were it not already able to experience something of future fulfillment, *RESPONSE*

In the mystery of the Incarnation, the Lord Jesus showed that God wishes to encounter us in our own concrete situation, *RESPONSE*

Active participation in the Eucharistic liturgy can hardly be expected if one approaches it superficially, *RESPONSE*

A heart reconciled to God makes genuine participation possible, *RESPONSE*

Fruitful participation in the liturgy requires that we be personally conformed to the mystery being celebrated, *RESPONSE*

The process of Christian formation is always centered on a vital and convincing encounter with Christ, *RESPONSE*

The initial encounter with Christ finds its source and summit in the celebration of the Eucharist, *RESPONSE*

A convincing sign of the effectiveness of Eucharistic catechesis is an increased sense of the mystery of God present among us, *RESPONSE*

No one eats that flesh of Christ without first adoring it; we should sin were we not to adore it (Saint Augustine), *RESPONSE*

In the Eucharist the Son of God comes to meet us and desires to become one with us, *RESPONSE*

Eucharistic adoration is the natural consequence of the Eucharistic celebration, which is the Church's supreme act of adoration, *RESPONSE*

Receiving the Eucharist means adoring him whom we receive, *RESPONSE*

The act of adoration outside of Mass prolongs and intensifies all that takes place during the liturgical celebration itself, *RESPONSE*

Only in adoration can a profound and genuine reception of the Eucharist mature, *RESPONSE*

The personal encounter with the Lord strengthens the social mission contained in the Eucharist, *RESPONSE*

Our personal relationship with Jesus present in the Eucharist points beyond itself to the whole communion of the Church, *RESPONSE*

Eternal life begins in us thanks to the transformation effected in us by the Eucharist, *RESPONSE*

The mystery of the Eucharist contains an innate power making it the principle of new life within us, *RESPONSE*

By receiving the Body and Blood of Jesus Christ we become sharers in the divine life in an ever more conscious way, *RESPONSE*

We are mysteriously transformed by the Eucharistic food, *RESPONSE*

Christ nourishes us by uniting us to himself; he draws us into himself, *Response*

Christianity's new worship includes and transfigures every aspect of life, *Response*

The Eucharist makes possible, day by day, the progressive transfiguration of believers to reflect the image of the Son of God, *Response*

There is nothing authentically human that does not find in the sacrament of the Eucharist the form it needs to be lived to the full, *Response*

The radical newness brought by Christ in the Eucharist permeates every aspect of our existence, *Response*

Eucharistic spirituality embraces the whole of life, *Response*

Today there is a need to rediscover that Jesus Christ is not an abstract idea but a real person, *Response*

The Eucharistic sacrifice nourishes and increases within us all that we have already received at baptism, *Response*

The sacrament of the Eucharist commits us to doing everything for God's glory, *Response*

The Eucharist provides the moral energy for sustaining the authentic freedom of the children of God, *Response*

Eucharistic communion includes the reality both of being loved and of loving others in turn, *Response*

The wonder we experience at the gift God has made to us in Christ gives new impulse to our lives and commits us to becoming witnesses of love, *Response*

We become witnesses when, through our actions, words and way of being, Another makes himself present, *RESPONSE*

The encounter with Christ in the Eucharist has become a communion of will, affecting even our feelings, *RESPONSE*

Each of us is called, together with Jesus, to be bread broken for the life of the world, *RESPONSE*

Every time we approach the Body and Blood of Christ in the Eucharistic liturgy, we also turn to the Blessed Virgin Mary, *RESPONSE*

Through the intercession of the Blessed Virgin Mary, the Holy Spirit renews our Eucharistic wonder, *RESPONSE*

It is for us to encourage one another to walk joyfully, our hearts filled with wonder, toward our encounter with the Holy Eucharist, *RESPONSE*

*Our Father...*

Most merciful Father, in the gift of the Holy Eucharist, your beloved Son has become my companion along the way. This great Sacrament contains the radical newness I so long for. May it penetrate every aspect of my life. Through the Body and Blood of Jesus Christ, allow me to become a sharer in the divine life in an ever more conscious way. Renew my Eucharistic wonder. Through Holy Communion make me a true witness of your Son so that, through my actions, words and way of being, Another will make himself present to the world. I ask this through Christ my Lord. Amen.

# Via Eucharistiae—
# The Way of the Eucharist

The *Catechism* teaches that the Eucharist is "the source and summit of the Christian life" (*CCC*, 1324, quoting *Lumen Gentium*, 11). The fact that the Eucharist is a "summit" suggests the image of an ascent leading us to that summit. The Way of the Eucharist is a devotion to the Holy Eucharist that resembles the Way of the Cross in its characteristics and format. The twelve "stations" represent some of the events in the life of Christ that bear a deeply Eucharistic dimension, in some way prefiguring the Sacrament of the Altar. The steps of the Way of the Eucharist anticipate and celebrate the consummate moment when Christ institutes the Eucharist at the Last Supper. We pray the *Via Eucharistiae* so as to deepen our understanding and appreciation of this great Sacrament of Charity and to enter into this Mystery with a total gift of self.

## THE FIRST STATION
### JESUS IS BORN IN BETHLEHEM

LEADER: O Sacred Banquet

ALL: In which Christ becomes our food, the memory of his Passion is celebrated, the soul is filled with grace and a pledge of future glory is given.

LEADER: You have given us Bread from heaven
ALL: Containing every blessing.

*"[King Herod] inquired of them where the Messiah was to be born. They said to him, 'In Bethlehem of Judea, for thus it has been written through the prophet:*
*"And you, Bethlehem, land of Judah, / are by no means least among the rulers of Judah; / since from you shall come a ruler, / who is to shepherd my people Israel."'"* (MATTHEW 2:4–6)

From the moment that Jesus Christ was born, the Mystery of the Eucharist was prefigured and anticipated. Jesus was born in Bethlehem—a name that means "House of Bread." The newborn Jesus was placed in a manger—in a vessel from which farm animals feed. As the shepherds came to kneel before their infant Savior in homage, it was as if they reclined at a table bearing a great Feast. The very posture of the baby Jesus in the manger bespoke his life's vocation: He was born to be our Bread of Life—in him we behold a heavenly Banquet. Silently from the manger, Jesus began to declare: Unless you eat my Body and drink my Blood, you will have no life within you.

The *Catechism* makes it clear to us that "only when Christ is formed in us will the mystery of Christmas be fulfilled in us" (*CCC*, 526). And how is it that Christ comes to be formed in us? That formation happens through the Sacrament of the Altar. When we enter into the mystery of Christmas, our appetite for our ultimate fulfillment is whetted. We hunger for Christ to be formed in us. Christ will be formed in us when the Eucharistic Christ is consumed by us. In Bethlehem, the House of Bread, we have found our Home.

Saint John Vianney once remarked that all the great longing of people throughout history, all the accumulated desire of the human heart was fulfilled in the crib at Bethlehem; God himself comes. Yet, once God comes and we recognize him as our ultimate fulfillment, immediately we are seized with fear and panic at the prospect that he might not stay, that his dwelling with us is only for a while. Having received such a presence, we cannot bear the thought of such an absence.

We crave this presence to be permanent. For we have waited for God-with-us all our life. That is why, from the first moment of his arrival, Jesus presents himself in a manner that proclaims that he is here for good. Lo, I am with you always, even until the end of the world. The Body of Christ that you see and adore in the manger will never leave you. It will continue to be given to you. As Christ progresses from this lowly cave to the Upper Room, Emmanuel will become yours in the Eucharist. Take heart! The Body you witness in worship in Bethlehem is the beginning of your forever.

### PRAYER

Loving Father, you sent your Son to satiate every longing of my weak yet longing heart. The Word became flesh at the Incarnation—flesh that your Son commands us to eat so that we may have the life we lack. As I meditate upon the Mystery of the Eucharist, give me new eyes to see how every aspect and action of Christ's life is meant to prepare me for the ultimate Communion he offers in the Eucharist.

## THE SECOND STATION
## JESUS FASTS FOR FORTY DAYS IN THE DESERT

LEADER: O Sacred Banquet

ALL: In which Christ becomes our food, the memory of his Passion is celebrated, the soul is filled with grace and a pledge of future glory is given.

LEADER: You have given us Bread from heaven

ALL: Containing every blessing.

*"Filled with the holy Spirit, Jesus returned from the Jordan and was led by the Spirit into the desert for forty days, to be tempted by the devil. He ate nothing during those days, and when they were over he was hungry."* (LUKE 4:1–2)

For what reason did Jesus, when he entered his forty-day sojourn in the desert, decide to forgo eating? There are many answers, but among them is certainly this: In the experience of hunger we discover things about our humanity that otherwise we could never know. Hunger shows us truths about ourselves. It humbles us. Hunger lays bare our limitations, our inabilities. It makes us surrender the fiction of self-sufficiency.

At the same time, hunger gives our life a refined focus, an intensified resolve. How much beauty in the world is the fruit of "hungry artists"? Hungry persons are those destined to depend, those who have no qualms about putting themselves at the mercy of others. The hungry person's survival itself depends on this depending. To be human is to *be* hunger.

Jesus was faced with a choice: Either he could satisfy his hunger by using his divine power to turn stones into bread, or he could hold fast to the humanity that his fast had enabled him to behold and freely depend all the more on his Father. To do anything but depend on the Father with the hunger that is our life would be to dally with the demonic. The aim of the Tempter's temptations was to persuade Jesus to renounce his Sonship, that is, his very identity. Christ knows that we are hunger. He knows how strong is the craving temptation in us to try to satiate our lives through self-reliance. The forty-day desert "school" taught Jesus what he must provide in order to save us from the temptation of trying to turn the stones of our life into bread that we presume will be the answer to our needs, our sufferings, our hardships. Self-made bread can never be enough for us.

The unfed Jesus quit the desert filled with the intention to feed us with a Bread that will save us from every temptation, a Bread that will transform every desert into a paradise, a Bread by which every crisis becomes a way to renew our claim on God the Father's love. For nothing delights the Father more than when his needy children come before him with such confidence. Empty of self, they are filled with expectation and an expectation he satisfies. Angels come to feed us with the Bread of Angels.

### PRAYER

Loving Father, the forty-day fast of your Son gave him an experience of humanity in its most needy and impoverished state. That need inspired Jesus to cling all the more to you. Give me this grace. I do not ask you to take away the neediness in my life, but rather to free me from every temptation by which I would trust an idol rather than you. May the fasting of my life increase my hunger for the Eucharist.

# THE THIRD STATION
## JESUS TEACHES THE LORD'S PRAYER

LEADER: O Sacred Banquet

ALL: In which Christ becomes our food, the memory of his Passion is celebrated, the soul is filled with grace and a pledge of future glory is given.

LEADER: You have given us Bread from heaven

ALL: Containing every blessing.

*"[O]ne of his disciples said to Jesus, 'Lord, teach us to pray just as John taught his disciples.' He said to them, 'When you pray, say: / "Father, hallowed be your name, / your kingdom come. / Give us each day our daily bread."'"* (LUKE 11:1–3)

The disciples of Christ watched Jesus, who was rapt in intense prayer. Then one of them mustered the courage to ask Jesus to teach them how to pray that way. They must have been wonderstruck at what the Lord told them.

For they were to pray with the confidence of sons and daughters, daring to call God "Father." And they were to ask the Father directly for their daily bread. But what exactly were they asking for in voicing that petition? Maybe the first disciples wondered: "Lord Jesus, in teaching us to pray, you tell us to beg the Father each day for our daily bread. But what is my 'daily bread?' Ever since the day I met you, I have come to look to you for everything. I have found in you a fullness that I never could have imagined until I saw your face. You alone have become what I depend on each day to keep going. You are the reason why I get out of bed in the morning and dare to take on ⁊

struggles of the day. Through my union with you I have been given the wisdom and strength to face all the trials and troubles of my life. Only in my companionship with you do I find the courage to confront the countless circumstances that seem to conspire against my happiness. You, Jesus, have become my very sustenance. I will obey what you command: I will pray each day for my daily bread. But secretly in my heart, as I make my petition, I will ask for a miracle: I will beg that somehow you yourself *become* my daily bread. For any bread that is not you is bread than cannot satisfy me.

What greater grace, what more astounding assurance is there than for you to become my actual nourishment? The fact that you instruct me to pray in this way makes plain that what I require to be myself, to live my life—not just to survive, but also to thrive, to live with joy and meaning and certainty—is something that I do not possess in myself. It must be given to me. I must use my freedom to beg for it. And so I beg, as you beg me to do. And the more I use my freedom to depend on the One who can provide my daily bread—who will become my daily bread—the freer I will become. Father, give us this day our daily bread. And let that Bread be your very Son."

### PRAYER

Lord Jesus, you teach me to pray for my daily bread in order to prepare my heart for the gift that you will offer at the Last Supper—your Body will become our daily bread, the Bread of Life. In asking for this daily bread, make the whole of my life a begging for you, and let me never settle for anything less than you and your love.

## THE FOURTH STATION
## JESUS ENCOUNTERS THE LEPER

LEADER: O Sacred Banquet

ALL: In which Christ becomes our food, the memory of his Passion is celebrated, the soul is filled with grace and a pledge of future glory is given.

LEADER: You have given us Bread from heaven

ALL: Containing every blessing.

*"A leper came to [Jesus] [and kneeling down] begged him and said, 'If you wish, you can make me clean.' Moved with pity, he stretched out his hand, touched him, and said to him, 'I do will it. Be made clean.'"* (MARK 1:40–41)

What transpired in Jesus the moment that he first laid eyes on a leper? Nothing could have saved him from the shock of what he saw. It was not just the leper's grotesque and repulsive disfiguration, the fetid, rotting flesh that stung Christ to his depths. It was the fact that, because of his ghoulish body, this human being was treated by the world like a monster, not a man.

Banned from the company of those who were "clean," he lived accursed and at a distance, alienated even from himself. Where did he find the strength to go on living? What held him back from despair? The hope that someday he would meet someone who would see beyond the loathsome appearance of his life, someone with an authority that would extend even to transforming his decrepit flesh. For someone—not himself!—had put such an expectation in his heart. So why shouldn't he live with the expectation that some day he would actually meet the one who filled his heart with this expectation so that that person could fulfill it? That expectation was what gave the leper hope. And it was that expectation that struck Jesus more than all the ghastliness he beheld.

For what the leper said was not a question; it was a statement: "If you will to do so, you can make me clean." That is, "Jesus, even despite the hideousness of my body, my vileness, my corruption, I see in you a correspondence with the longing of my heart that no disease can contaminate or take away. I know you are the One I have been waiting for. I know you have the power to make the putrid pure. And I know that, if you will it, it will happen. And I just want you to know that all of my life, although I have no right to do so (for I am unclean), I have been begging for you to come close to me."

And then something happened to the leper that had never happened before in his life: Someone touched him. And the leper's flesh became perfectly pristine—he was like a child again. If this is what could happen if Christ gave one man back his flesh, what would happen if Christ gave the whole world his own flesh in the Eucharist? Go, show yourself to the great High Priest whom you will find in the Sacrament of the Altar.

### PRAYER

Lord Jesus, so often I feel like the leper—isolated and alone, faced with impossible circumstances, overwhelmed by sorrows. But in my heart lives an expectation that exceeds all my misery. You are the one who corresponds to my heart. If you will to do so, you can fill my life with your presence. In all confidence I place myself in homage before you.

## THE FIFTH STATION
## THE MULTIPLICATION OF THE LOAVES AND FISHES

LEADER: O Sacred Banquet

ALL: In which Christ becomes our food, the memory of his Passion is celebrated, the soul is filled with grace and a pledge of future glory is given.

LEADER: You have given us Bread from heaven

ALL: Containing every blessing.

*"Taking the five loaves and the two fish, and looking up to heaven, [Jesus] said the blessing.... They all ate and were satisfied.... Those who ate were about five thousand."* (MATTHEW 14:19–21)

One of the most crippling effects of original sin is our insistence on making ourselves the measure of all things. It infected the disciples as Jesus prepared to feed the five thousand. They became overwhelmed by the limitations of the circumstances: The crowd was huge; the place was deserted; the provisions were nil; the time was late. For them the most reasonable solution to this predicament would have been to dismiss the people and send them off to fend for themselves. But the unity that had formed because of their following of Christ was too precious to imperil; Jesus had his people sit down on the grass and stay together. The same thing happened some time later when the Lord fed the four thousand (see Matthew 15:32–39), but the disciples had not learned their lesson. They got completely exasperated with Jesus when he refused to send the people away. In a fit of frustration, they complained to Christ, "How could we ever get enough bread to satisfy such a huge crowd in such a deserted place?"

They saw the situation; they saw reality from their own limited measure. And the minute that reality became something they could not control, they panicked. Christ worked these miracles not just to feed the multitudes but also to convert such a starving attitude, which leaves us famished before the wiles of the world. For we were made with a desire for the Infinite. But at times fatalism gets the better of us. We become pessimistic before what seems impossible to us. And whenever we reduce our desire for the Infinite to what we are able to do ourselves, we reduce what Jesus Christ is able to do in our lives. The miracles of multiplication make plain that Jesus Christ is the only true measure of our life. Then, every impossible situation is resolved, but never in a way that is "just enough." Always with God we are left with a lavish bounty.

Soon after, a similar miracle with a loaf of bread took place in an Upper Room. Sadly, it would then be the disciples themselves who disperse, deserting Jesus and going off by themselves. But not for long. What happened to them in the miraculous bread of the Eucharist brought them back together again as Jesus' people. For the Eucharist became the culmination of the Infinity they once tasted in a deserted place. And the effect of that Food did not permit them to live according to any lesser measure.

## PRAYER

Lord Jesus, save me from the trap of making myself the measure of all things. When faced with circumstances that are trying or beyond me, please move me to do what you do: to look to your

Father in heaven filled with unshakeable confidence and trust. Nothing delights you more than the chance to feed us when we are languishing. Nothing glorifies you more than when your people depend on you for everything. Let me live by the measure of the miracle of the Eucharist.

## THE SIXTH STATION
## JESUS DELIVERS THE BREAD OF LIFE DISCOURSE

LEADER: O Sacred Banquet

ALL: In which Christ becomes our food, the memory of his Passion is celebrated, the soul is filled with grace and a pledge of future glory is given.

LEADER: You have given us Bread from heaven

ALL: Containing every blessing.

*"Jesus said to them, 'Amen, amen, I say to you, unless you eat the flesh of the Son of Man and drink his blood, you do not have life within you.'... Then many of his disciples who were listening said, 'This saying is hard; who can accept it?'... Jesus then said to the Twelve, 'Do you also want to leave?' Simon Peter answered him, 'Master, to whom shall we go? You have the words of eternal life.'"* (JOHN 6:53, 60, 67–68)

These words of Jesus—"Unless you eat my Body and drink my Blood you will not have life within you"—at first hearing come across as both terrifying and insane—the ranting of a madman. Based on that assessment, some of Christ's disciples recoiled, repudiated him and refused to remain in his company any longer.

But not Simon Peter. Why? It is true that on their own the words that Jesus spoke in the Bread of Life discourse strike the ear as preposterous. But the point is that, thanks to the call of Christ, we are no longer on our own. Everything about our life has changed as a result of our companionship with Christ, especially the way that we conceive of ourselves, the way that we conceive of events that happen, the way that we conceive of reality itself. In these words Jesus is preparing us for the greatest Newness of all—the Newness that will come in the Eucharist—something that we could never conceive of apart from Jesus. Yes, based on our own inadequate preconceptions, these words seem absurd.

But Simon Peter decided that he was not going to judge these words based on his own limited understanding. Rather, he was going to judge this most daring claim of Christ based only on his experience of being with Jesus. And what that review revealed was this: ever since the first moment that Peter had been with Jesus, Peter's life had changed for the better. He had experienced joy, self-possession, conviction, peace; he had witnessed the impossible happen; he had heard the Father speak from the heavens. And that experience taught him that the most reasonable thing he could do in moments of crisis or confusion would be to trust Jesus rather than trust his own way of looking at things. For never—not once—had remaining close to Christ let Peter down. Simon Peter heard these shocking words of Jesus Christ; he remembered what staying close to Jesus had produced in his life; and he made this judgment, saying with rock-solid certainty: "To whom shall we go? You alone have the words of life. You. As insane as it may sound, I'm staying."

If the event of the Mystery made flesh is true, "then all aspects of life…must revolve around it. And it is precisely man's perception of being undermined, no longer being the measure of his own self, that places him in the position of refusal."[2]

## PRAYER

Lord Jesus, in this inconceivable declaration—"Unless you eat my Body you will have no life within you"—you give me a new way to conceive. Save me from being a slave to my own weak and fallible understanding. When I am in doubt about the ways you offer to come into my life with your fullness, let me remember my companionship with you and the way it always transforms my life in ways I never could have conceived of.

## THE SEVENTH STATION
## JESUS TELLS THE PARABLE OF THE PRODIGAL SON

LEADER: O Sacred Banquet

ALL: In which Christ becomes our food, the memory of his Passion is celebrated, the soul is filled with grace and a pledge of future glory is given.

LEADER: You have given us Bread from heaven

ALL: Containing every blessing.

*"And he longed to eat his fill of the pods on which the swine fed, but nobody gave him any. Coming to his senses he thought, 'How many of my father's hired workers have more than enough food to eat, but here am I, dying from hunger. I shall get up and go to my father.'"* (LUKE 15:16–18)

The Prodigal Son opted for a desperately foolish course of action in pursuit of his own happiness. In effect extorting his would-be inheritance from his father (an action that suggested how much he anticipated his father's death), the son "disowned himself" from his family. Moreover, he immigrated to a distant, foreign country. By so doing he demonstrated his desire to cut himself off from his own nationality, his ethnic roots. Also, as a Jewish person who willingly consented to work on a pig farm, he renounced his own religion. So once he had squandered his money on dissolute living, the Prodigal Son was poor in every possible sense: He had no family; he had no fatherland; he had no faith, he had no funds. Is any greater destitution possible?

Yet, indigent as he was, the Prodigal Son still possessed something priceless, something with power to make him rich. What he still owned was his heart. No degree of impoverishment could take that away.

Quite the contrary, our experience of being without only makes the yearnings of our heart more poignant, more insistent. There, in the personal squalor he had created for himself, the Prodigal Son came to his senses at last. "Coming to our senses" means listening to the desires of our hearts without prejudicing them, denying them, manipulating them, reducing them. It means paying attention to our heart without any distractions. For our heart is made to lead us back to the Father. Only in the Father will we find the happiness that our heart craves. What is the grace that enabled the Prodigal Son to rediscover the counsel of his heart and to follow it no matter the cost? His hunger. On account of the Prodigal Son's hunger, he came to his senses at last. Through the experience of hunger, the

Prodigal Son realized that the most reasonable thing he could do was return to his father. Through the experience of hunger, the Prodigal Son saw a way out of the catastrophe that he had wrought in his life. And, thanks to his hunger, he finally had the clarity to see the one who totally corresponded to the cravings of his heart.

Christ understands how effective hunger is for realigning our priorities, for reorienting us to our ultimate happiness, our destiny. In the parable of the Prodigal Son, the Lord highlighted the instrumental role that hunger plays in saving those who are lost so that when we find ourselves in those same straits we will know where to turn: the Eucharist.

## PRAYER

Lord Jesus, let me come to my senses at last—let me see how all the hungers of my life lead me to the Father through you. Save me from whatever would distract me from returning to the Father again and again in my life. May I value my spiritual hunger as a mercy that makes me crave for what truly corresponds to my heart: Your presence in the Eucharist.

## THE EIGHTH STATION
## JESUS ENCOUNTERS THE SAMARITAN WOMAN AT THE WELL

LEADER: O Sacred Banquet

ALL: In which Christ becomes our food, the memory of his Passion is celebrated, the soul is filled with grace and a pledge of future glory is given.

LEADER: You have given us Bread from heaven

ALL: Containing every blessing.

*"Jesus answered and said to her, 'If you knew the gift of God and who is saying to you, 'Give me a drink,' you would have asked him and he would have given you living water.'... Jesus answered and said to her, 'Everyone who drinks this water will be thirsty again; but whoever drinks the water I shall give will never thirst; the water I shall give will become in him a spring of water welling up to eternal life.'"* (JOHN 4:10, 13–14)

The human reality that drew the Prodigal Son back to his father was hunger. And the human reality that made the Samaritan woman at the well open and receptive to an enemy she would otherwise repulse was thirst. The prospect of finding a definitive solution to her chronic thirst moved the woman to disregard her disdain for this Man in favor of paying attention to him.

This is the grace of spiritual thirst in our life: it quiets all our protests and prejudices in its quest for Living Water that will quench it. Christ always comes to us in the criticalness of our human condition, in the powerlessness of the circumstances and the crises over which we have no control. Jesus Christ acknowledged the woman's natural thirst, and through the woman's encounter with Jesus she came to recognize her own deeper, supernatural thirst. Without her thirst, would she have cared or dared to listen to Jesus?

The experience of physical thirst makes us aware of a thirst within us that goes beyond our bodies, a thirst that can be slaked only by the Beyond in a drink which itself is an imbibing of the Infinite. "Every man is searching for a passion worthy of filling his soul to capacity."[3] It is our thirst that sparks that search for passion; it is Christ's Passion that fills our thirsty souls to overflowing. The nineteenth-century author Monsignor Robert Hugh Benson wrote:

> There come moments and even periods in our lives when religion becomes an intolerable burden; when the search is so long and fruitless that we sicken of it.... At times like this we lose heart altogether. It seems to us even that our own desires are not worth satisfying; that religion...reaches an end beyond which there is no going; that we are not even ambitious of attaining heaven.... It is when we are wearied out then by desiring, when desire itself has failed, that Jesus speaks to us.[4]

He says: "Take this and drink from it: this is the cup of my Blood." Two chapters earlier in the Gospel of John, Jesus turned six jars of water into a hundred gallons of wine. There Jesus demonstrated his lavish tenderness to guests who were thirsty, and here he showed the same pity to a most-parched soul. The Lord begs us not to fear our thirst—it will lead to his open side on the cross from which will flow blood and water to satisfy us.

### PRAYER

Lord Jesus, may I see in my thirst a craving for something that I cannot satisfy. Let my thirst lead me to you, the Living Water. May I abandon every attempt to orchestrate and engineer my life. All that you ask is that I give you something to drink—what you desire is my self-surrender, my trust, my obedience, my faith. Take it—it is yours.

# THE HEALED LEPER GIVES THANKS TO CHRIST

LEADER: O Sacred Banquet

ALL: In which Christ becomes our food, the memory of his Passion is celebrated, the soul is filled with grace and a pledge of future glory is given.

LEADER: You have given us Bread from heaven

ALL: Containing every blessing.

*"As [the lepers] were going they were cleansed. And one of them, realizing he had been healed, returned, glorifying God in a loud voice; and he fell at the feet of Jesus and thanked him."* (LUKE 17:14B–16)

When the healed leper returned to the presence of the Lord and fell at his feet to offer his first words as a pure man—words of profound thanksgiving—Jesus Christ was moved. He witnessed how much the man needed this opportunity to offer thanks in order for his healing to be complete. The Lord recognized that if this miraculous work of mercy were to be left unacknowledged by gratitude, the man's cure would be lacking in some way. Through the leper's offer of thanksgiving, he was able to continue on his way, not just with disease-free flesh, but also with a relationship with the One who makes all things new.

Every miracle is meant to lead to that relationship, and it is thanksgiving that cements it. In commenting on the other nine lepers who fail to return to Jesus to offer thanks for their cure, Saint Leo the Great made a key point. He said that, even if they had attained bodily health, those nine did not have spiritual health because they were lacking in this duty of reciprocity. The healed leper offers the presence of his pristine flesh to Jesus as his offer of thanksgiving to him. Perhaps in that gesture Jesus foresaw a way for all people always to render fitting thanksgiving to God.

The Eucharist is a thanksgiving. United in the sacrifice of Christ, we offer the flesh and blood of Jesus to the Father as the consummate act of gratitude to God. As the leper with his clean flesh clung to the feet of Christ, we in our weakness cling to the Eucharistic flesh and blood of Jesus in the hope that God will regard our gratitude and be pleased. The reason why we can be thankful in the first place is because God has given us hearts made for gratefulness.

But none of us wants to contract leprosy in order to get a heart as great and grateful as the healed leper's. So we beg the Lord to let us see plainly the mercy that he instills in each transfiguring moment of our life. As we go on our way, may we constantly recognize the newness in our flesh that is there because of the compassion of Jesus Christ. May it send us back thankful to his flesh in the thanksgiving of the Eucharist. Let us give thanks to the Lord. It is right to give him thanks and praise.

### PRAYER

Loving Father, it is our duty and our salvation always and everywhere to give you thanks through your beloved Son, Jesus Christ. Cleanse me of all my ingratitude, my complacency, my presumption. May every great grace and little miracle of my life send me back swiftly in thanksgiving to the presence of your Son.

## THE TENTH STATION
## CHRIST INSTITUTES THE EUCHARIST AT THE LAST SUPPER

LEADER: O Sacred Banquet

ALL: In which Christ becomes our food, the memory of his Passion is celebrated, the soul is filled with grace and a pledge of future glory is given.

LEADER: You have given us Bread from heaven

ALL: Containing every blessing.

*"[Jesus] said to them, 'I have eagerly desired to eat this Passover with you before I suffer.... Then he took the bread, said the blessing, broke it, and gave it to them, saying, 'This is my body, which will be given for you; do this in memory of me.' And likewise the cup after they had eaten, saying, 'This cup is the new covenant in my blood, which will be shed for you.'"* (LUKE 22:15, 19–20)

On the night he was betrayed, Jesus thanked his Father, broke the bread, and, in effect, told his disciples, "When first we began, I told the crowds, 'Blessed are those who hunger and thirst for holiness—they shall have their fill.' Now you will understand the truth of these words. You, Andrew—the first thing you asked me when we met was, 'Rabbi, where do you stay?' because you wanted to stay with me. So did the leper, once I had healed him. So did the adulterous woman when everyone else decided to go away. So did the Gerasene demoniac, once he had been freed from his demons. So did the scribe who declared, 'Teacher, wherever you go I will come after you.' And blind Bartimaeus, with his eyesight restored—the first thing he did was follow me up the road. You saw it. You are witnesses.

"To be close—in my presence—meant more to each of them than even their healing, the miracles they had received. What had they found? What happened to them? It was what moved those four faith-filled friends to hoist the dead weight of their paralyzed companion up the side of a building, remove the tiles of the roof and lower the paralyzed man through the hole into my presence. Why take such a risk? What made it worth such a sacrifice? What happened to the Samaritan woman at the well that compelled her to leave her water jar behind, to race off into town and bring the entire population out to meet me?

"And what was their request? You were there; you heard it. 'Stay with us,' they begged. 'Stay.' And you, Simon Peter—it seems so long ago—after that miraculous catch of fish you confessed yourself a sinner and begged me to leave you. But you clung so tightly to my knees that it was impossible for me to take a single step. Not that I would have or wanted to. For I have come to sinners to call sinners. And you said to me later, 'Lord, to whom shall we go?' You stayed even when others believed no longer. Something more than what you could understand kept you with me. So tonight I tell you, you whom I call my friends. My friends: It is not you who want to stay with me; it is I who want to stay with you. To be with you always, until the end of the world. Take this, all of you, and eat it. This is my Body—my self—which will be given up for you."

## PRAYER

Lord Jesus, the whole of your life is the offer of a presence without which I cannot live. The sacrament of the Eucharist assures me that you are always close, that you are always offering me your friendship. Enable me to live my life as an obedience to your Body and Blood that you offer in sacrifice out of love for me.

THE ELEVENTH STATION

## THE WOMEN KEEP VIGIL AT THE TOMB OF JESUS

LEADER: O Sacred Banquet

ALL: In which Christ becomes our food, the memory of his Passion is celebrated, the soul is filled with grace and a pledge of future glory is given.

LEADER: You have given us Bread from heaven

ALL: Containing every blessing.

*"When the sabbath was over, Mary Magdalene, Mary, the mother of James, and Salome bought spices so that they might go and anoint him. Very early when the sun had risen, on the first day of the week, they came to the tomb."* (MARK 16:1–2)

The women came to the tomb of the crucified Son of God. They came in a spirit of profound reverence, as those who approach a tabernacle for Eucharistic adoration. They came with the intention of making contact with the flesh of Jesus Christ. That was why in their hands they bore vessels of spices for anointing. Even in death they were drawn to the Lord's Body.

Even in death they lived from the certainty that the only place to be is close to where Christ is. In this they showed themselves to be exquisite theologians. The *Catechism* teaches that "during Christ's period in the tomb, his divine person continued to assume both his soul and his body" (*CCC*, 630). They intuited this truth—that the Person they once encountered in the trials and problems and sins of their lives was still there with them and that the way to that Person continued to be through his flesh. They were certain that the encounter had not ended. And so they went while it was still dark, when the sun was just rising, because the only way to counteract the world's oppressive darkness is by drawing near to Christ the Light.

So great was their desire to be close again to the One whose intimacy had changed every dimension of their life that they went without forethought about who would move the stone. Nonetheless, they did not turn back. It was more important for them to be at a tomb that was closed than to risk closing in on themselves at a distance from Jesus. The women approached the tomb filled with expectation.

Maybe their hope is that which is expressed by Johann Sebastian Bach in his *St. Matthew Passion*:

Make thee clean, my heart, from sin;
I would my Lord inter....

May He find rest in me,
Ever in eternity,
His sweet repose be here.
World, depart; let Jesus in![5]

The women desired to identify their very selves with the tomb of Christ, so great was their certainty that their communion with Christ was not over. Their action prefigures the gesture of all those whose faith moves them to present themselves before the reserved Blessed Sacrament. From these women who stand as patron saints of Eucharistic adoration, we learn how to keep vigil before the presence of the Lord filled with expectation, certainty and desire.

The women found the stone moved, the tomb empty. Every time the tabernacle door is opened, the stone is rolled away again, joy ignites and resurrected life comes forth.

## PRAYER

Lord Jesus, when it seems that we have failed, that everything is over, and we are in the darkness of the tomb with Christ, then the angels will come and roll away the great heavy stone, and resurrection with Christ will come. May my Eucharistic adoration before your tabernacle renew my certainty and hope. (Based on the writings of Caryll Houselander.)

## THE TWELFTH STATION
## THE DISCIPLES ON THE ROAD TO EMMAUS ENCOUNTER CHRIST

LEADER: O Sacred Banquet

ALL: In which Christ becomes our food, the memory of his Passion is celebrated, the soul is filled with grace and a pledge of future glory is given.

LEADER: You have given us Bread from heaven

ALL: Containing every blessing.

*"But they urged him, 'Stay with us, for it is nearly evening and the day is almost over.' So he went in to stay with them. And it happened that, while he was with them at table, he took bread, said the blessing, broke it, and gave it to them. With that their eyes were opened and they recognized him."* (LUKE 24:29–31)

Cleopas and another disciple of Jesus Christ one evening after Easter were making the seven-mile journey on foot from Jerusalem to the village of Emmaus. They did not notice how strenuous their long walk was because they were caught up in a lively exchange, discussing all the events that had transpired in Jerusalem over the past few days. So engrossed were they in conversation that they remained oblivious to a fellow traveler who stepped up beside them on the road and began to walk along with them. They did not recognize this man who asked, "What are you discussing as you go along your way?"

Who did not know the events surrounding the death of Jesus? But the question was not so simple. For it was the disciples themselves who were acting in ignorance of the events of Christ. To this perfect stranger they made a confession about their flagging faith: "We were hoping that Jesus would be the one to set Israel free." If they had truly known the Event who is Jesus, their hope would not have been in such a state of decay. At the Last Supper the Lord commanded his disciples, "Do this in memory of me."

To memorialize Jesus is to unite ourselves to his saving self-sacrifice in such a way that the redeeming Event of Christ's love becomes present, informing our every thought, word and action. It is the Eucharist that makes this re-happening of Christ's saving Presence possible right to the inner core of things.

But these two disciples had let their memory of Christ erode. And so the risen Christ reinitiated the encounter with them in a Eucharistic way. He became their companion. He spoke words that made their hearts burn, words that recalled the consummate words of the Last Supper: "This is my Body. It will be given for you. I will shed the Blood that will inaugurate a new and everlasting covenant. Through the shedding of my Blood, your sins—all sins—will be forgiven." And he reenacted a gesture—so simple and yet so profound—whose significance was unforgettable: He broke bread.

Then they recognized him, in the breaking of the bread. The Event was no longer an idea, a concept; it had become flesh! It was a Person. It was a presence that freed them from the decay of themselves and awakened them. Jesus then vanished, and the disciples' forgetfulness of Jesus vanished, too. The two disciples rushed back to Jerusalem to continue the encounter with the others.

### PRAYER

Lord Jesus, you give us the Eucharist to win us back from the worries and preoccupations that so damage our hope. Let me live the memory of your presence. Deepen my love for you in the breaking of the bread so that I will never doubt that you are with me always. Stay with me.

# *Notes*

### EUCHARISTIC MEDITATIONS
### FOR EACH DAY OF THE MONTH

1. Albert Einstein, quoted at http://tow.charityfocus.org.
2. Catherine of Siena, *The Dialogue*, Suzanne Noffke, trans. (New York: Paulist, 1980), p. 54.
3. Antonin Gilbert Sertillanges, O.P., *Spirituality*, Dominican Nuns of Corpus Christi Monastery, trans. (New York: McMullen, 1954), p. 176.
4. Alfred Delp, as quoted in Pope Benedict XVI, *Jesus of Nazareth*, Adrian J. Walker, trans. (New York: Doubleday, 2007), p. 33.
5. Massimo Camisasca, *Together on the Road: A Vision of* Lived Communion *for the Church and the Priesthood* (Boston: Pauline, 2005), p. 89.
6. Lucinda Franks, "Miracle Kid," *The New Yorker*, May 1999, http://209.85.173.104.
7. Sofia Cavalletti, *The Religious Potential of the Child: Experiencing Scripture and Liturgy with Young Children*, Patricia M. Coulter and Julia M. Coulter, trans. (Chicago: Liturgy Training Publications, 1992), p. 126.
8. David Cairns, trans., *The Memoirs of Hector Berlioz*, quoted in Kay Redfield Jamison, *Touched With Fire: Manic-Depressive Illness and the Artistic Temperament* (New York: Free Press, 1993), pp. 19, 20.

9. Pär Lagerkvist, "Evening Land /Aftonland," W.H. Auden and Leif Sjoberg, trans. http://theologytoday.ptsem.edu.

10. Dorothy L. Sayers, *Spiritual Writings* (Boston: Cowley, 1993), p. 93.

11. Quoted in Father Luigi Giussani, "How a Movement Is Born," August 1989, www.clonline.org.

12. Cardinal Joseph Ratzinger, *Pilgrim Fellowship of Faith: The Church as Communion*, Henry Taylor, trans. (San Francisco: Ignatius, 2005), p. 110.

13. Homily on Saint Agatha by Saint Methodius of Sicily, bishop, *Liturgy of the Hours*, vol. 3 (New York: Catholic Book, 1975), p. 1365.

14. Pope John Paul II, Message to Meeting of Communion and Liberation, August 20, 2002, Zenit.org.

15. Louis Lavelle, *The Dilemma of Narcissus*, W.T. Gairdner, trans. (Burdett, N.Y.: Larson, 1993), p. 55.

16. Helen Keller, *The Story of My Life* (New York: Bantam, 1990), p. 16.

17. Cardinal Joseph Ratzinger, *Principles of Catholic Theology: Building Stones for a Fundamental Theology*, Sister Mary Frances McCarthy, S.N.D., trans. (San Francisco: Ignatius, 1987), p. 52.

18. Luigi Giussani, *Why the Church?* Viviane Hewitt, trans. (Montreal: McGill-Queen's University, 2001), p. 15.

19. Luigi Giussani, "Religious Awareness in Modern Man," *Communio*, vol. 25, no. 1 (Spring 1998).

20. Cardinal Joseph Ratzinger, *God and the World: Believing and Living in Our Time*, Henry Taylor, trans. (San Francisco: Ignatius, 2002), p. 26.

21. J.R.R. Tolkien, *The Letters of J.R.R. Tolkien*, Humphrey Carpenter, ed. (Boston: Houghton Mifflin, 1981), p. 53.

22. Cavalletti, p. 89.

23. Cavalletti, pp. 70–71.

24. Flannery O'Connor, "A Temple of the Holy Ghost," in *The Complete Stories* (New York: Farrar, Straus and Giroux, 1971), pp. 247–248.

25. J.R.R. Tolkien, *The Fellowship of the Ring* (New York: Ballantine, 1994), p. 415.

26. www.oprah.com.

27. Cardinal Joseph Ratzinger, *God Is Near Us: The Eucharist, the Heart of Life*, Henry Taylor, trans. (San Francisco: Ignatius, 2003), p. 29.

28. Ratzinger, *God Is Near Us*, p. 126.

## EUCHARISTIC REFLECTIONS
## ON THE MYSTERIES OF THE HOLY ROSARY

1. Ratzinger, *God Is Near Us*, p. 105.

2. Catherine of Siena, *The Dialogue*, p. 122.

3. Byzantine Ramblings, http://209.85.165.104.

## EUCHARISTIC DEVOTIONS

1. Pope Benedict XVI, *Sacramentum Caritatis*, Apostolic Exhortation on the Eucharist as the Source and Summit of the Church's Life and Mission, February 22, 2007, introduction, www.vatican.va.

2. Luigi Giussani, *At the Origin of the Christian Claim*, Viviane Hewitt, trans. (Montreal: McGill-Queen's University, 1998), p. 105.

3.  Lavelle, p. 200.

4.  Robert Hugh Benson, *The Friendship of Christ* (Westminster, Md.: Newman, 1955), p. 141.

5.  Johann Sebastian Bach, *St. Matthew Passion* (Hamburg: Polydor International GmbH., 1984), pp. 119, 121.